WILD WOMEN

WILD
WOMEN

Crusaders, Curmudgeons, and Completely Corsetless Ladies in the Otherwise Virtuous Victorian Era

AUTUMN STEPHENS

Conari
Press

CORAL GABLES

Cover Design: Jayoung Hong
Layout & Design: Morgane Leoni
Cover Photo: © everettovrk / Adobe Stock

For permission requests, please contact the publisher at:
Mango Publishing Group
2850 S Douglas Road, 2nd Floor
Coral Gables, FL 33134 USA
info@mango.bz

For special orders, quantity sales, course adoptions and corporate sales, please email the publisher at sales@mango.bz. For trade and wholesale sales, please contact Ingram Publisher Services at customer.service@ingramcontent.com or +1.800.509.4887.

Wild Women: Crusaders, Curmudgeons, and Completely Corsetless Ladies in the Otherwise Virtuous Victorian Era

Library of Congress Cataloging-in-Publication number: pending
ISBN: (print) 978-1-64250-364-7, (ebook) 978-1-64250-365-4
BISAC category code HIS058000, HISTORY / Women

Printed in the United States of America

To my mother, Yvonne Stephens,
and to Leigh Barton, Margaret Crane,
Bernadette Luciano, and
Cathryn Stephens Marsh—
the wildest women I know

CONTENTS

A Word to the Reader — 7

Flamboyant Flirts and Lascivious Libertines — 11

Tough Lovers and Fiery Sirens — 19

Brazen Brides and Wicked Wives — 31

Twisted Sisters and Mortifying Mothers — 43

Maidens à la Mode — 52

Hatchet Queens and Pistol Packers — 60

Dreaded Desperados and Gutsy Gamblers — 70

Radical Rescuers and Militant Feminists — 84

Fearless Frontierswomen — 96

Audacious Artists and Ad Hoc Architects — 106

Shocking Scholars and Wanton Wordsmiths — 118

Controversial Curers and Ingenious Invalids — 132

Alarmingly Litigious Ladies — 147

Outrageous Orators and Sassy Suffragists — 153

Rabble Rousers and Muckrakers — 165

Holy Terrors and Pope Perturbers — 174

Shameless Exhibitionists and Notable Narcissists — 182

Scandalous Socialites and Hell-Raising Heiresses — 191

Southern Rebels and Capital Offenders — 204

Totally Transcendent Travelers — 212

Bibliography — 216

About the Author — 223

A WORD TO THE READER

Every era, it seems, selects one definitive snapshot of femininity to paste into its collective scrapbook. The plain, practical Puritan and the gin-nipping flapper; robust Rosie the Riveter and waifish, wraith-like Twiggy; the billowing, buxom Gibson Girl and the beaded, barefoot earth mother—each has found a cherished place in the museum of national memory. And in those archetypal albums, the pages titled "Victorian" are entirely given over, of course, to portraits of the Lady. There she sits amid the bric-a-brac of her cluttered parlor or poses prettily with her children, her eyes never quite meeting ours, oddly stiff-spined and somber for all the pretty fripperies and furbelows of her costume.

And indeed, that prim progenitor didn't have much reason for risibility. Burdened by pounds of petticoats and corseted within an inch of her life, the exertion of cracking a smile might easily have cracked her spine. Proscribed by convention (and in many cases, by law) from pursuit of professional endeavors, she was shunned by society for even the slightest breach of domestic decorum. Contemporary etiquette manuals prescribed the manner in which she should request the loan of mourning attire, remark on the aroma of a rose, and recover from a swoon—not to mention an endless list of situations which should inspire her to faint in the first place. And according to one guardian of feminine virtue, it even behooved her to segregate the works of male and female authors on her bookshelves. ("Their proximity," it was noted, "unless they happen to be married, should not be tolerated.")

Astonishing as that preoccupation with propriety seems by today's standards, it was not entirely devoid of a certain cultural logic. In both the United States and its cousin across the Atlantic, the era to which virtuous Victoria (queen of England from 1837 to 1901) gave her name was distinguished above all by the increasing industrialization of society.

In response to the advent of a dehumanizing machine age, a cult of domesticity arose, with the home as the temple, and the "Angel of the Hearth" as high priestess of that rarefied realm. But, as many a luckless Lady found, her kingdom was considerably more circumscribed than that of Victoria, and her pedestal was in effect her prison. "Woman should not be expected to write, or fight, or build, or compose scores," proclaimed Ralph Waldo Emerson in 1841; "She does all by inspiring man to do all." Three years later, *Godey's Lady's Book* chimed in with another caveat against careers: "There is nothing more dangerous for a young woman," declared that popular periodical in 1844, "than to chiefly upon her intellectual powers, her wit, her imagination, her fancy." And by 1870, Britain's matronly monarch had added her powerful voice to the censorious chorus, thundering from her throne for the world "to join in checking this mad, wicked folly of 'Woman's Rights' with all its attendant horrors on which her poor feeble sex is bent."

There was, of course, only one Victoria (even if it did sometimes seem during the course of her sixty-four-year reign that she was destined to rule forever). But in fact, there were many Victorian Americas, few of them truly fit for a proper lady to inhabit. During that genteel epoch, the United States would experience the horrific upheaval of the Civil War, a vast surge of westward migration into uncharted new territories, a bitter half-century struggle for suffrage, and an increasing feminization of the nation's work force. And during those decorous decades, American women leapt from their pedestals left and right, defying their passive sisters in the parlor to play a role in the great dramas of the day.

THE WOMAN WHO SET THE TONE FOR AN
ENTIRE CENTURY

In San Francisco, a courtesan appeared as a plaintiff in court, suing her clients for fraud; in Montana, a laundress in her seventies decked a gentleman who refused to pay his bill. A forty-three-year-old schoolteacher plunged down Niagara Falls in a wooden barrel, and a frail lighthouse keeper pulled twenty-two sinking sailors out of the ocean off Rhode Island. A pair of Colorado madams fought a public pistol duel over their mutual beau, and two lady lovebirds were legally wed in Michigan. An ad hoc abolitionist spirited away scores of slaves on the Underground Railroad, while a secessionist spy swallowed a secret message as she was arrested, claiming that no one could capture her soul. And long before Geraldine Ferraro was a twinkle in her great-grandmother's eye, one power-meister ran for president on an equal rights platform, while another hopeful head of state flaunted her faith in Communism and free love.

Wise or wicked, flamboyant or foolhardy, indomitable or insufferable—no single word can characterize the scores of nineteenth-century women who lived life on their own terms (and often, it must be added, paid an extravagant price). But clearly the faded cameo of the lovely listless Lady no longer serves as an accurate likeness. Here, then, with apologies to Queen Victoria (as well as a bow to all our brave, brazen foremothers who didn't give a fig for her fantasies about femininity), are a few alternative images to round out the Victorian photo album.

FLAMBOYANT FLIRTS AND LASCIVIOUS LIBERTINES

Adah Menken (1835–1868)
Enigmatic Equestrienne

Galloping through the California desert one sultry day with poet Joaquin Miller, mysterious, mystical Adah Menken suddenly dismounted and flung herself to the ground. "I was born in this yellow sand," she sighed dramatically, "sometimes and somewhere...in the deserts of Africa, maybe..." In anyone other than the muscular muse of nineteenth-century bohemia, this curious behavior might have been deemed a serious breach of dating protocol and possibly even cause for medical concern. But in the magnificent Menken (sometime actress, sometime poet, always fascinatingly flaky), it was utterly enchanting. "Who could forget that graceful yellow figure...in a single garment of yellow silk?" Miller sighed.

Who, indeed? No one, perhaps, except those who preferred other minimalist ensembles modeled by Menken in her most famous stage role, that of a rather horsey Russian price. Clad variously in a flesh-colored leotard, gauzy maillot, or thigh-skimming tunic, Menken dazzled audiences from Paris to Peoria when she leapt onto a snorting stallion and stormed up a dizzyingly steep mountain pass. Critics disagreed as to the degree of physical danger involved in the stunt—that theoretically treacherous incline was after all fashioned from cardboard. But no one could deny that the voluptuous young horseman's attire posed grave risks to gentlemen prone to cardiac arrest.

Certainly young Mark Twain appeared to have lost his heart. A "magnificent spectacle dazzled my vision," he wrote, "flaming out of the heavens like a vast spray of gas-jets." "Such calves!" exclaimed a Nevada writer, much taken with Menken's sturdy legs; "They were never reared on milk." A Parisian journalist became obsessed by her large pink nostrils, which, he marveled, "open and shut like the nostrils of a war horse." Even the poet Swinburne couldn't refrain from rhapsodizing about Menken's "beautiful passionate body" in a way that suggested, rather self-servingly, that he knew what he was talking about.

But if "The Naked Lady" seemed spontaneously to ignite the flame of masculine desire, the reverse was also true. Four times a wife and rumored (albeit often by themselves) to be mistress to a host of leading literati, she bared her soul as brazenly as her body. "He attracted me physically," she remarked of her second spouse, a prizefighter more skilled in the martial arts than marital ones. Still, the seductress in saffron did not cop to any common brand of lust. "In much the same fashion," she asserted with astonishing certainty, "…Mark Antony's ardent embraces stirred the tiger-blood in Cleopatra's veins." Even on her deathbed, Menken managed to cut a ravishingly romantic figure, succumbing slowly to tuberculosis in a Parisian garret in her thirty-third year. To scores of aesthetically astute admirers—among them Charles Dickens and Alexandre Dumas—her premature demise was to come as a great blow. But the conspicuous consumptive herself took a more cosmic view. "After all, I have lived more than a woman of a hundred years," she consoled one teary-eyed young artist. It wasn't the literal truth, of course. But somehow it made perfect poetic sense.

"Thou knowest."
—*Inscription on A.M.'s tomb*

Aimée Crocker (1862–1941)
Dangerous Liaisons

"Flirtation...can be the most fascinating pastime in the world," gushed California railroad heiress Aimée Crocker. Indeed, by the age of sixteen, the voluptuary vixen had already tumbled for a German prince "who had the most romantic saber scars" and a Spanish toreador ("his touch left scars on my soul"). To the great relief of San Francisco society columnists, Crocker's wounds healed quickly and she went on to hula *à deux* with King Kalakaua of Hawaii, jitterbug through the jungles of Borneo with a bona fide headhunter, and hootchy-kootchy her way into the harem of the Rajah of Shikapur.

Nor did adventurous Aimée, five times a bride, feel compelled to curtail her bed hopping during bouts of matrimony. Consequently, her marriages tended toward the rather abbreviated variety. It is after all one thing for a sophisticated spouse to shut his eyes to a love triangle; another altogether to overlook a veritable polytetrahedron of passions. Even the most peripheral paramour, however, seldom proved completely problem free—particularly the type who naively featured himself as leading man rather than best supporting actor. Ah well, that was simply the gaucheness of youth. "They all get over husbands, given half a chance," giggled Crocker.

As to whether the quintet of unfortunate grooms (including a Russian prince almost forty years her junior) who wed the wealthy wanderlust-victim ever got over *her*, Crocker wasn't much concerned. "Husbands, at best, have little to do with 'people,' " she sniffed; "I know, because have had a certain number of them."

Indeed, by the time she sat down to write her memoirs at the age of seventy-four, the cultured coquette had "had a certain number" of almost everything, including some truly bizarre bedfellows. Not that she deigned to bat an eye when a boa constrictor slithered into her boudoir one night and proceeded to do as boas do, enveloping her body in a snug cross-species hug. In fact, it seems Crocker found the reptilian rendezvous quite a turn-on: "He gave me a strange tickling sensation that was, I confess, very enjoyable."

FANCY A NAP WITH THIS BEDFELLOW?

Still, for the professional flirt, the conquest is vastly more compelling than its consequences. Another seduction successfully completed, Crocker was soon snoozing away as the smitten snake, still coiled about her, lay staring into the dark. "It was like being in the strong embrace of a man," shrugged the world-weary party girl; "I was more than comfortable."

"Things always happen to me."

—A. C.

An Old-Fashioned Cure

Despite its title, Dr. Mary Jacobi's *The Question of Rest for Women During Menstruation* didn't read like any quaint Victorian period piece. In that 1876 treatise, which netted the prominent physician a prestigious prize from Harvard University, she argued that celibacy constituted a leading cause of cramps. Unlike more mainstream MDs, Jacobi also maintained that ladylike indolence led to invalidism. But under certain circumstances, it seemed, a retreat to the boudoir was just what the doctor ordered...

Victoria Woodhull (1838–1927)
Sexual Politics

By her own admission, virtue was not a significant selling point for Victoria Woodhull, the nation's first female presidential candidate. Indeed, the leading light of the Equal Rights party made no bones about her shocking sexual orientation. "I am a free lover!" she boasted in 1871. Lest the Victorian electorate find itself unclear on that rather avant-garde concept, Woodhull went on to enumerate a few of her pet passions: pleasure without procreation, sex without spouses, and prostitution without imprisonment. "They say I have come to break up the family," she smirked; "I say amen to that with all my heart." And with a nod toward her chagrined cohabitant, she added, "When I cease to love him, I will leave him."

Whatever other accusations the moral majority might sling at the candid candidate, no one could claim she pandered to traditional taste. In 1868, however, Woodhull evidently did encourage her sister Tennessee Claflin, a shapely séance artist, to ensnare the aging Cornelius Vanderbilt in a lucrative affair. Soon the mesmerized millionaire had entered into an unholy alliance not only with Tennessee, but with the brokerage firm of Woodhull, Claflin & Company, which made its dazzling Wall Street debut in 1870. Known as the "Bewitching Brokers," the scheming sisters managed to clear $700,000 in profits before Cornelius recalled certain preexisting family obligations and withdrew, taking his invaluable insider information with him.

"While others argued the equality of woman and man, I proved it by successfully engaging in business," Woodhull would later note. As to the source of her rather unethical expertise, however, she was intelligent enough not to specify. Indeed, if consistency is the hobgoblin of small minds, this creative capitalist's mental faculties were of the most capacious order. "Christ was a Communist of the strictest sort, and so am I, and of the most extreme kind," she informed the nation, and proved her point by publishing the first American version of Karl Marx's *Manifesto*.

In one particular, however, Woodhull's campaign proved drearily conventional: the country concentrated its attention on her scandalous sex life and largely ignored her political views. "My judges preach against 'free love' openly, and practice it secretly," she complained, and retaliated by penning an article about a well-known minister's adulterous affair. But the counterattack did more damage to Woodhull's credibility than to that of the clergyman, and it will come as no surprise to students of history that she did not prevail in the election of 1872. In fact, even had the female portion of the population been permitted to vote that year, the racy radical still would not have been able to cast a ballot in her own favor. She passed election day in jail, held on charges of sending obscene material through the mails, and General Ulysses S. Grant, the manly military hero of Appomattox, ascended to the presidency. Then as now, America just couldn't get that excited about a candidate who was more interested in making love than war.

"Believing as I do that the prejudices which still exist in the popular mind against women in public life will soon disappear, I now announce myself as candidate for the presidency."

—V. W.

Kate Chopin (1851–1904)
Fiction's Filthiest Female

"It was the first kiss of her life to which her nature had really responded," ran a particularly purple passage in *The Awakening*, Chopin's now widely acclaimed (but back then, too, too naughty) turn-of-the-century novel. "It was a flaming torch that kindled desire."

Clearly, the fictional Mrs. Pontellier—a middle-aged mother dabbling in the dangerous waters of adultery—had been waiting a long time for that blowtorch buss. As it happened, the audacious author had also been waiting a long time to describe it. Having produced a half-dozen babies during her first decade as a wife, Chopin found that diapering duties kept her from dipping into the inkwell at will. Not until she was nearly forty did she publish *At Fault*, an entirely innocuous (and entirely unremarkable) first novel. By the time *The Awakening* appeared nine years later, however, she had churned out more than one hundred stories for such entirely reputable magazines as *Vogue* and *The Atlantic* and had forged a formidable national reputation in the local-color genre. But judging by the orgy of outrage which greeted her steamy second novel in 1899, both the promiscuous Mrs. Pontellier and the prolific Mrs. Chopin would have done well to keep their pantalettes on for another half-century or so.

"This is not a pleasant story," sniffed one repressed reviewer; "*The Awakening* is too strong a drink for moral babes, and should be labeled 'poison,' " thundered another. In St. Louis, Chopin's own hometown, the book was banned from the library and its author banished from the Fine Arts Club. even critics who praised her sensuous prose couldn't help lamenting that "so beautiful a style and so much refinement of taste" had been squandered "on an essentially vulgar story."

Long before Chopin-bashing became fashionable in literary circles, however, neighbors had their suspicions about the wanton writer. Rumor had it that she received guests while soaking in her bath, puffing languorously on Cuban cigars throughout such sudsy social calls. And after the death of her husband in 1882, the still-winsome widow evidently accepted the nocturnal sympathy of numerous gentlemen, not all of whom were bachelors. In short, hissed one acid-tongued acquaintance, Chopin was—those infamous interpersonal ablutions notwithstanding—"a *dirty* lady." And, this acquaintance hinted darkly, "You don't know *all* that she did."

Well, yes and no. Based on Chopin's apparently well-researched portrayal of physical passion, a few vivid images certainly spring to mind. Nor, according to one late-nineteenth-century survey of female sexuality, was she the only "torpid, torrid, sensitive blossom" ever to ripen into orgasmic bloom in an American boudoir. Still sleeping off a nasty puritanical hangover, however, the nation just wasn't ready to wake up and admit it could smell the coffee. Greatly affected by the chilly reception accorded her scorching masterpiece, the exasperated X-rated writer seldom picked up her pen between the publication of *The Awakening* and her death five years later. "Sometimes I feel as if I should like to get a good, remunerative job to do the thinking for some people," she sighed.

"Oh! Talk of me if you like, but let me think
of something else while you do."

—K. C. (in *The Awakening*)

TOUGH LOVERS AND FIERY SIRENS

Laura Fair (1837–1919)
In Love and War

For lovely Laura Fair, a fluffy Southern belle who drifted west trailing a string of dead or damaged husbands behind her, romance was a lot like target shooting. Practice, it seemed, made perfect—and in her opinion, it never hurt to pack a pistol. Let cute little Cupid claim his victims with arrows of tenderness: on the adults-only battlefield of love, chunks of hot lead constituted the *coup de grâce* of choice.

Then again, Fair's checkered background didn't precisely encourage the notion that love was any pastime for sissies. She first hit the great rifle range of matrimony at the impressionable age of sixteen; within a year, her spouse had perished under most mysterious circumstances. Husband Number Two skidded from the cooing-dove stage to the stupid-turkey stage in just six short months. "He would shoot over the head of my bed, sir, with a pistol," Fair testified at the divorce trial. "Then he would go out and shoot the poultry in the yard, fifty at a time, one after another." A better sport (and perhaps a better marksman), Number Three left the birdshot alone, but blew himself out of the water when Fair made it clear she preferred to loll in some other guy's featherbed.

At this point, a less ambitious adventuress might have thrown in the matrimonial towel, resigning herself to a lifetime of narrow cots and charitable works. Not so Fair, who gamely snapped up the proposal of Alexander Crittenden, a prominent San Francisco lawyer, six months after their starry-eyed meeting in 1863. Numerous clichés and misdemeanors, however, were to mar that ill-fated romance, starting with Crittenden's startling confession that his wife did not understand him. Naturally, this revelation came as something of a shock to Fair, who had not previously realized her fiancé was married. Nor did a three-way meeting of wife, mistress, and middleman result in the sort of amicable French arrangement Crittenden had evidently hoped to broker. Not to worry, the adulterous attorney promised his ladylove, a divorce was definitely in the offing.

But after seven more years of sharing her still-married sweetheart with his spouse, fed-up Fair saw she'd have to take the separation into her own hands. "You have ruined me!" she explained, and shot her procrastinating paramour through the heart. Some things never change. At Fair's sensational murder trial, witnesses for the prosecution provided numerous interesting yet irrelevant details of amorous encounters with the accused. A damsel so depraved as to enjoy a fulfilling sex life, it was implied, was doubtless guilty of far worse, and the trigger-happy temptress was sentenced to hang.

Women's rights crusaders (among them Elizabeth Cady Stanton and Susan B. Anthony, neither a known libertine) breathed a sigh of relief when the Supreme Court overturned Fair's death sentence on the basis of insanity. But it was muttered in some suffragist circles that the rationale was all wrong. In an era when a woman's worth was defined by her marital status, was it so crazy for a long-suffering lady to give romance her very best shot?

"I did it and I'm glad."

—L. F.

The Tenacious Tenderfoot

Footloose Adah H. Anderson wasn't the first American to make a spectacle of herself during the late-nineteenth-century mania for walking marathons. She was, however, the only individual to continuously circumnavigate the Mozart Theater in Brooklyn for twenty-eight days straight, revealing in the process (as the *New York Times* noted) "a fair amount of leg." This rather exhibitionistic exercise, incidentally, was not entirely without purpose: Ms. Anderson walked away with $10,000 from her sponsors for successfully completing the feat.

Lillie Hitchcock Coit (1843–1929)
Incendiary Ingenue

Pledged to wed some fifteen times before her twentieth birthday, San Francisco socialite Lillie Coit, née Hitchcock, deftly handled the problem of simultaneous betrothals by alternating her engagement rings from day to day. Among her romantic rejects, noted an awestricken acquaintance, were "a prince, three or four British lords, and the scion of one of those old Dutch families in New York." But California's most fickle fiancée never did warm to the tepid advances of those aristocratic admirers. The flame of her passion for a local volunteer fire company known as Knickerbocker Engine No. 5, by contrast, burned bright and true. At the sound of fire bells, lovely Lillie abandoned all pretense of decorum—and on one notable occasion, a wedding rehearsal—and streaked off to help her beloved Knicks battle a blaze.

Possibly Coit's pyric predilection ran in the genes: Mom, a transplanted Southern belle, had personally torched her ancestral home to thwart "white trash" squatters following the Civil War. Or perhaps it was merely the proverbial appeal of gentlemen in uniform—especially the sort of uniform featuring a manly length of fully functional hose. (Appropriately enough, San Francisco would one day erect Coit Tower, a very vertical monument indeed, in honor of its favorite fire fetishist.) In any event, Coit was so taken by the brave boys of No. 5 that she had all her lingerie, Freudian and otherwise, embroidered with their insignia.

LILLIE'S MONUMENT TODAY IN SAN FRANCISCO

Moved by her devotion (or perhaps her utter wackiness), the company adopted her as its mascot. The kooky coquette, in turn, adopted the masculine vices of playing poker and drinking bourbon. "There isn't another woman in all San Francisco as unladylike as you," scolded one of her few gal pals. "Shush," retorted Mrs. Coit, taking another indecorous drag on her cigarette; "You must be forgetting yourself." Her ardor for aberrant behavior quite undampened, she went on to carouse at cockfights and prowl the seedy waterfront bars, and she once amused herself by hosting a violent boxing match at the exclusive Palace Hotel. Thought the referee begged to declare a draw, the pugilistic party girl wasn't satisfied until the loser sprawled unconscious on the floor, his blood slowly seeping into the rich Oriental carpet.

Naturally, a mother worries. "You are preparing to go to the devil," sparked Mrs. Hitchcock on one incendiary occasion. But to Firebelle Lil (who would, in fact, relish every scandalous step of her progress toward the realm of burning brimstone), Hades sounded like quite a hoot. "Preparations are unnecessary," she proudly informed her parent; "He's been expecting me this many a day."

> "Men are like tea—the real strength and goodness are not properly drawn until they have been in hot water."
> —L. H. C.

Mattie Silks (1848–1929)
Duel Ownership

"A most disgraceful row occurred late on Friday night," trumpeted the *Denver News* in September 1877. "Two notorious women of the town, Mattie Silks and Katie Fulton, were principals..." The egregious incident—so the *News* noted—occurred when, pursuant to a very liquid afternoon picnic, rival resort owners Silks and Fulton decided to engage in a formal pistol duel in Denver Park. Each, it seems, was determined to prove her claim to the comely Mr. Cortez Thompson. In fact, each was evidently fully (though perhaps only fleetingly) prepared to die for his love.

Denverites in the know, however, didn't need the *News* to provide them with the dirt on the dueling madams. Silks, the classic blowsy blonde, had embarked upon her chosen career at the age of nineteen. For a full quarter of a century, she was to rule over a trio of the city's poshest parlorhouses with a plump yet powerful fist. Unfortunately, she neglected to keep an equally tight rein on Thompson, a gambler who maintained his fine athletic figure by footracing. Beautiful of body but weak of will, Bit Mattie's man just couldn't say no when Fulton (like Silks, a long-term fixture on the local brothel scene) made a play for him. Unable to amicably resolve their personal property dispute—and with the tongue-tied Mr. Thompson apparently unable to speak for himself—the competing courtesans saw little choice but to haul out the heavy artillery.

On the fateful day, Fulton scored the coup of being seconded by Thompson himself, while Silks made do with a gentleman named Thatcher. An additional ten or twelve participants were also in attendance as third-stringers. Possibly owing to their intoxicated condition, however, neither madam managed to get off an accurate shot, and the backups were forced to amuse themselves by engaging in minor fisticuffs. Thompson, by contrast, acquitted himself admirably in the role of *homme fatale*, neither swooning at the sound of gunfire nor shrieking when he suffered the only injury of the day—a bullet burn to the neck, which as the *Denver News* assured its readers, was "not regarded as serious."

Evidently Fulton's interest in Thompson was as transitory as the trauma to that gentleman's skin, for she bowed out of the picture soon after the inconclusive duel. Without the threat of competition, Silks saw no reason to rush the course of romance; she didn't get around to making an honest man of her heartthrob until 1884. Nonetheless, she treated the blushing bridegroom most solicitously, first taking him on a European honeymoon, then escorting him to the Klondike, where she planned to support him in her customary style. Regrettably, however, Mr. Thompson's constitution proved too fragile for the rough Yukon climate, and he perished soon thereafter, a thing of beauty and joy to the end.

"Some of us are becoming the men we wanted to marry."

—Gloria Steinem

Cordelia Botkin (1853–1910)
Candy Was Dandy

She was a soft-spoken California housewife who wanted more out of
life than a set of silver candy dishes and didn't mind stepping out on
her spouse to get it. He was a hard-living Associated Press reporter
who liked a spot of fun now and again, so long as his wife didn't
suspect. For six steamy years, Cordelia Botkin and sweetie John P.
Dunning feasted in secret on the fruit of forbidden love.

Then one day Dunning announced it was time to say adios to amour—
he'd lost his appetite for illicit trysts. In fact, he informed Botkin,
he was soon to set sail for Puerto Rico, where he planned to pursue
his career as a foreign correspondent. Reading between the lines,
his distressed mistress could only conclude that Mrs. Dunning had
discovered the dalliance and issued some sort of marital ultimatum.

The year was 1898, and contemporary etiquette manuals offered
precious little guidance to abandoned adulteresses. Nonetheless,
well-bred Botkin knew better than to stoop to any truly tacky form
of self-expression, like plugging her paramour with bullets. Besides,
her aim was to eliminate the competition, not the prize. Under the

circumstances, only the most decorous form of retaliation would do. Hence the beautiful little box of chocolates (daintily bound in a lace hankie) which soon turned up in the mail of the long-suffering Mrs. Dunning. Not until it was entirely too late did the victim of Botkin's very Victorian crime suspect just how much thought had gone into those well-doctored delicacies—nor, obviously, how much arsenic.

Even in the nineteenth century, drop-dead manners didn't make a big impression in criminal court; the charming *chocolatière* was quickly convicted of murder and sentenced to life in prison. Far from languishing in the sallow halls of San Quentin, however, Botkin soon sweet-talked her way into a private suite replete with luxuriant bedding. On occasion, her adoring jailers treated her to a shopping spree in San Francisco's most elegant emporia (though one presumes, naturally, that they kept her far away from the candy counters). Nor was the standard jailhouse slop deemed fit fare for a person with such a refined palate; instead, the privileged prisoner was permitted to order her meals from restaurants. The killer dessert of Botkin's own creation—those infamous bye-bye bonbons—never appeared on the murderess' menu, however. She perished in 1910, not after dinner, but following a lingering malady characterized by the rather poetically minded coroner as "softening of the brain, due to melancholy."

"Love never dies of starvation, but often of indigestion."
—Ninon de Lenclos

Violent Passions

Like many a spurned suitor, nineteen-year-old Alice Mitchell didn't know quite what to say when fickle Freda Ward returned her ring and called off their affair. Eventually, however, Mitchell managed to give voice to her feelings by slitting her former fiancée's throat. "I killed Freda because I loved her," she explained at her murder trial in 1892. Apparently it never occurred to her to just say it with flowers...

Jennie Rogers (1844–1909)
Undying Love

Professional girlfriend Jennie Rogers was always looking for a few good men, and usually they were looking for her, too. A showy six-footer with a weakness for fast horses and fancy clothes, she wasn't hard to spot. Nor, with the exception of one noteworthy occasion when a straying swain found himself staring at the business end of her revolver, was she difficult to get along with. By the time she hit Denver in 1879, the popular paramour's romantic resumé included stints as a doctor's wife, steamboat captain's sweetheart, live-in lover of the mayor of Pittsburgh, and a permanent position as steady girl of the St. Louis chief of police.

Not every kept woman aspires to sin on a grand scale; a more complacent coquette might have been content to pursue that horizontal career path indefinitely. But by the age of thirty-six, this ambitious mistress had outgrown the role of glorified housekeeper and was heading up a house of her own. "Everything First-Class," Rogers assured potential patrons in the *Denver Red Book: A Reliable Dictionary of the Pleasure Resorts of Denver*. And indeed, her shiny new "Hall of Mirrors" (located in cozy proximity to the Colorado capitol building) reflected the faces—as well as other interesting parts of the anatomy—of some of the West's most prominent politicians. "Each afternoon about three o'clock, the august lawmakers would retire to Jennie Rogers'...and there disport themselves in riotous fashion," a neighbor would later recall. "Nothing was thought of that sort of thing in those days."

As for Ms. Rogers' own code of personal conduct, suffice it to say an equally lax standard prevailed—at least when her St. Louis lawman wasn't in town. Like her carefree clientele, the brassy beauty evidently saw no reason to bestow her favors on just one member of the opposite gender. She did, however, take the precaution of underwriting a career change for secret heartthrob Jack Wood, installing the young hack driver in a Salt Lake City saloon far from the beat of her official boss.

Long-distance love being what it is (and Jack being a rambunctious rascal some twenty years her junior), the result was perhaps all too predictable. In 1888, Rogers showed up in Utah with romance on her mind, only to discover her two-timing youth in the arms of another woman. what was good for the goose was apparently not at all salubrious for the gander; in a fit of pique, the maddened madam pulled her pistol and let the bullets fly.

Whether she aimed to kill or merely to stun, no one can say; fortunately, there were no fatalities. In fact, Rogers' violent expression of primal passion appears to have acted as quite a powerful aphrodisiac. Not only did Jack recover from his wounds, but he also got his priorities in order and managed to resolve his issues concerning commitment. In August 1889, the happy couple tied the knot, giving a very newfangled twist to the term *shotgun wedding*.

> "I shot him 'cause I love him, God damn him!"
> —*Tessie Wall (Murderous Madam from California)*

Julia Bulette (1832–1867)
Too Good to Be True

When dazzling, diamond-encrusted *demimondaine* Julia Bulette came scorching into Virginia City in 1859, worried wives and decent dowagers averted their eyes when she passed in the street. "That whore will come to a bad end," predicted one smug Christian soul, not at all displeased by the prospect. For the moment, however, the proprietor of Nevada's most popular new pleasure palace (who, it was rumored, charged a staggering thousand dollars a night for her services) showed no signs of ill health. Scarlet ostrich feathers and sable scarves trailing, she streaked through town in a lacquered carriage drawn by two gleaming white ponies. The daily stage from San Francisco brought to her door bouquets of fresh-cut flowers and fancy trinkets from the toniest San Francisco boutiques. And through that exclusive doorway sauntered some of the state's most solvent gentlemen, drawn by the rare opportunity to sample French cuisine, fine champagne, and all of the other decadent delights of parlorhouse legend.

What truly irritated the virtuous women of Virginia City, though, was the fact that the flamboyant madam apparently led the good life in more ways than one. "Her skin may be scarlet, but her heart is white," claimed an admirer blessed with unusual visual acuity. Nonetheless, the local ladies did not care to hear their husbands run on about how Bulette had played Florence Nightingale to a crew of ailing miners, dispensing soup and sympathy instead of her more customary favors. Reports of her fundraising efforts for the Union likewise failed to impress—even patriotism, it seems, did not render a prostitute any more palatable. Naturally, no God-fearing woman wished to know which specific acts of generosity, financial or otherwise, warranted Bulette's honorary membership in the Virginia City Engine Company No. 1. And in 1861, when the firefighters picked the "Queen of Sporting Row" as princess of the annual Independence Day parade, a thick cloud of self-righteous smoke settled over many a formerly happy home.

Nor did Bulette's untimely demise in 1867 (just as predicted, she met a most unsavory fate, succumbing at the age of thirty-five to the violent assault of a jewel thief) fully clear the air. To his astonishment, the jailed strangler found himself an instant cause célèbre among the gentlewomen of Virginia City, who plied him with fried chicken and homemade pies and pleaded passionately for his pardon. Quite uncharitably, many of those upright homemakers also expressly forbade their grieving menfolk to pay final respects to the murdered madam. But once again, marital mandate was to no avail: though the funeral day dawned drizzly and bleak, scores of defiant male mourners, led by Engine Company 1, followed Bulette's casket from church to cemetery. Meanwhile, peering through the narrow slats of semi-closed shutters, their indignant spouses maintained a vigilant watch over the whole dismal affair. Even in a state of rigor mortis, they suspected, the best bad woman in the West was up to no good.

"It's always the finest fruit that the birds pick at."

—Lillie Hitchcock Coit

Beyond the Pale

In the pursuit of perfect pallor, some Victorian vixens consumed small doses of arsenic. British actress Lilly Langtry, on the other hand, took her beauty sleep with a slab of raw veal resting on her face. (Presumably this was intended as a boon to the complexion rather than a culinary shortcut.) It is not known, however, whether the curious custom was in any way connected with Langtry's subsequent purchase of a California stock farm in the late nineteenth century.

BRAZEN BRIDES AND WICKED WIVES

Lucy Stone (1818–1893)
The Name Game

The very liberated Lucy Stone demanded neither bobos nor bouquets from beau Henry Blackwell. Nor did she set much stock in pretty prattle about love and devotion. But that didn't make the well-known women's rights lecturer, whose address at the Worcester women's suffrage convention in 1850 converted Susan B. Anthony to the cause of feminism, an obvious matrimonial mark for any lazy Lothario. As her sensitive suitor well knew, no out-of-date macho mate would ever win the heart of Stone.

"A wife should not more take her husband's name than he should hers," the semiotically astute suffragist had taken pains to inform him; "My name is the symbol of my identity and must not be lost." Under the circumstances, Blackwell thought it best not to try to make a conventional Mrs. out of his unconventional inamorata. "I wish, as a husband, to *renounce* all the privileges which the law confers upon me, which are not strictly *mutual*," he insisted; "Surely *such a marriage* will not degrade you, dearest."

But thirty-five-year-old Stone, who had vowed to "call no man master," didn't cave in so quickly. No longer the naïve schoolgirl who blamed the chauvinist cadences of the Bible on faulty translation, she had long since learned to take neither competent interpreters nor her own equality for granted. Only after a two-year barrage of Blackwell's politically correct platitudes was she persuaded to merge her destiny—though not, of course, her surname—with that of her fellow feminist.

Just as the obliging groom had promised, the Stone-Blackwell nuptial ceremony in 1855 conspicuously omitted any retro reference to wifely obedience. Indeed, Blackwell didn't even buss his bride until she had delivered herself of a lengthy manifesto of matrimonial independence: This act on our part implies no sanction of...such of the present laws of marriage as refuse to recognize the wife as an independent, rational being," she informed the assembled guests; "We believe that personal independence and equal human rights can never be forfeited."

By all accounts, the unconventional union was a mutually satisfactory one, no doubt further enhanced by the fact that the wary wife maintained her own private bank account (and on occasion, her own private residence). Having already inspired an ever-enlarging circle of "Lucy Stoners" to retain their maiden names after marriage, the separate-but-equal spouse emerged as a full-blown cause célèbre when in 1858, she declined to pay property taxes on her New Jersey home. Since neither she nor any other American woman had the right to vote, Stone asserted, the fees assessed constituted "taxation without representation."

DEFINITELY LUCY STONE

Then as now, government officials received gratuitous refresher courses on the principles of democracy with ill grace; they retaliated by seizing and selling several pieces of her furniture. One doubts, however, that Stone lost much sleep over the loss of a few sticks of wood. Their value, after all, was entirely inconsequential when compared to that of her good name.

> "My name is Lucy Stone, nothing more. I have been called by it for more than sixty years, and there is no doubt whatever about it."
>
> —L. S.

Mary Mahaffey (dates unknown)
The Fraudulent Fiancée

Fortune hunter Mary Mahaffey certainly wasn't the first woman in the world to marry for money. Without a doubt, however, the Nevada City party girl was one of the few who have ever made a mockery of matrimony solely in order to finance one single soirée. Perhaps she didn't actually *intend* to ensnare a certain wealthy rancher in the web of her charms during a trip to Sacramento in 1850. Nonetheless, common courtesy would have dictated at least a cursory mention of her common-law spouse back at home. Blissfully unaware that she was already handsomely outfitted in the husband department, however, the lovestruck landsman pressed his suit. And when Mahaffey whispered that she was his and his alone, he promptly plunked down three hundred dollars for her trousseau.

Naturally, Mahaffey's closest companions—a rather loutish lot of drunks and roustabouts, it seems—were pleased to learn of her betrothal. Indeed, they proved eager as a bevy of bridesmaids to bring the engagement to a felicitous conclusion. Gambler Jack White, for example, agreed to pose as a minister, a service for which he charged the feckless fiancé only fifty dollars. In the guise of town clerk, a salon proprietor issued a mock marriage license, extracting another ounce of gold from the husband-to-be. And a pair of local bartenders set their shot glasses aside just long enough to issue a raft of romantic last-minute invitations: *A rancher from Bear River will be spliced to Mary Mahaffey this evening… You are wanted for to be there, for Mary would feel bad if you wasn't. PS No guest will have to kiss the bride if he doesn't want to…*

On December 31, 1850, pseudo-parson White solemnly pronounced the couple man and wife, pursuant to which two hundred celebrants tucked into a lavish wedding feast accompanied by all the customary libations. Perhaps contemplating other traditional nuptial delights that awaited him, the giddy bridegroom settled the thousand-dollar tab without so much as a blink.

Needless to say, he never received the expected return on his investment. As one of the guests who enjoyed both an excellent meal and a good giggle at the expense of that ill-fated gentleman recorded in his journal: "After the sucker was thus fleeced, his Deary told him he was a fool." And, she added, if he didn't quit the premises immediately, "she would shoot him with a pistol she flourished." Having thus disposed of the gullible groom, Mahaffey rejoined the revelers, and one assumes, went on to enjoy the wedding night of her dreams.

"A fool and his money are soon married."

—Carolyn Wells

Charlotte Cushman (1816–1876)
Risqué Role Model

Apparently *amore* among the ladies was more common in the nineteenth century than one is usually led to believe—not that it was acknowledged at the time. in the half-closed eyes of one biographer, cross-dressing Charlotte Cushman was not only "a great actress," but one "who also abided by the Victorian code of womanly behavior." Never mind that this exemplar of feminine propriety (considered in her day to be America's foremost actress) preferred the role of leading man to leading lady, declaiming her lines in a "hoarse, manny voice." Never mind that during her retirement in Rome, she presided over a frisky gaggle of gals known as the "Jolly Female Bachelors," many of whom were not at all averse to doing more or less as the ancient Greeks did. "A brief girlhood engagement and a short-lived love affair in 1836 exhaust her romantic history," prevaricated the cautious chronicler, who evidently preferred appeasing reactionary readers to rendering an accurate portrait of his subject.

On one point, however, that glib gentleman was entirely correct: Cushman's amorous career—which constituted something of a one-woman support-the-arts program—might indeed be termed exhaustive. Over the years, her private collection of close female companions would come to include a painter, a poet, an actress, and one or two sculptors. But if the personal details of the Boston-bred thespian's life were carefully concealed from history, her public persona was an open book to those who cared to read between the lines.

A VERY ROMANTIC ROMEO

"I was born a tomboy," proclaimed the girl who grew up to portray several famous men, including Hamlet, Romeo, and Claude Melnotte. Debuting in drag in Albany in 1837, Cushman courted her Capulet to "enthusiastic applause." In proper Philadelphia, on the other hand, the spectacle of a rounded Romeo cozying up to her leading lady did not arouse unbridled approbation; Cushman had, in the view of an oddly unimaginative fellow actor, entirely "unsexed" herself, thereby destroying "all interest in the play." But by 1845, sophisticated London audiences couldn't get enough of the miss who played Montague at the Haymarket. "Miss Cushman is a very dangerous young man," exclaimed one Brit, much impressed by her prowess with a sword. "Just man enough to be a boy," sighed another. Even when Cushman's own sister was cast as Juliet, the worldly Europeans didn't so much as arch an eyebrow. Indeed, one starry-eyed reviewer, terming Romeo "ardently masculine" and his incestuous inamorata of the stage "tenderly feminine," ventured his opinion that the polarized pair should rightfully be married at once.

Fortunately, it was not to her sibling but to a subsequent Juliet that Cushman (aptly described by one critic as "the most successful Romeo I have ever seen") was eventually wed. Or so reported poet Elizabeth Barrett Browning, who noted in 1852 that the allegedly nonamorous actress and colleague Matilda Hays had agreed to a "female marriage." "They have made vows of celibacy and eternal attachment to each other," explained Browning, who confessed that she found the arrangement somewhat irregular. But the friend to whom she related the gossip was not at all taken aback. "Oh, it is by no means uncommon," she yawned.

> "No actress should ever marry at all, or if
> she does, she should quit the stage!"
> —C. C.

Sarah Borginnis (1813–1866)
The Biggest Bigamist

Frequently married and seldom divorced, camp follower Sarah Borginnis neither wanted nor needed a man to take care of her. Robust, redheaded, and nearly six feet tall, the powerfully-build patriot, who made a career out of catering to the special needs of the nation's enlisted men, was more than capable of handling her own affairs. "You son-of-a-bitch," she once bellowed to a cowardly doomsayer as she proceeded to send him sprawling in the dust; "You just spread that report and I'll beat you to death!"

But when it came to bureaucratic red tape, even brazen Mrs. Borginnis found her hands tied. It seems the US Army took the official position that single women constituted a dangerous distraction to soldiers; only in the company of a spouse were the ladies welcome to tag along with the troops. Thanks to this peculiar proviso, Borginnis was already a wife three or four times over. But when she applied for permission to march out of Mexico with the Army in 1848, no one seemed to care that neither death nor dissolution had ever punctuated the intervals between her previous bouts of martially induced marital bliss. All that the Army required was an on-premises Mister, pronto.

Evidently well-schooled in the art of guerrilla husband-hunting, Borginnis lost no time in getting to the point. "Who wants a wife with $15,000 and the biggest leg in Mexico?" she called out as she galloped into the departing ranks. "Come on, my beauties...who is to be the lucky man?" After pondering this rather generic proposal for some time, Trooper Davis of Company E shyly declared his interest in both loot and limb. But the feckless fiancé insisted he wanted the ceremony done civilian style, with "a clergyman here to tie the knot." Smirked Borginnis, "Bring your blankets to my tent tonight and I will learn you to tie a knot that will satisfy you."

But seemingly Davis proved an inept student, for the union soon came unraveled, and Borginnis abandoned her final spouse at the US-Mexico border. Apparently eluding human bondage for the rest of her life, she died a more-or-less single woman in 1866, receiving a magnificent military funeral with full honors for her contributions to the US Army.

"I've married a few people I shouldn't have, but haven't we all?"

—Mamie Van Doren

The Wandering Wife

Nevada prospector Henry Comstock bought his bride fair and square from her former husband—sixty dollars and a horse sealed the bargain. But it seems that Mrs. Comstock never really settled into the spousal role. Just a few days into her second round of matrimony, she ran off with a gentleman characterized by one historian as "a seductive youth from Carson City." It didn't take Henry long to track down his mate, and she amiably agreed to wander no more. No sooner was her husband's back turned, however, than she clambered out a window and fled with her lover once again. the next time Henry caught up with the pair, he instilled the fear of God in the "seductive youth," and his sixty-dollar woman consented to stay with him through the winter. By spring, however, Mrs. Comstock was gone for good, having absconded with "a long-legged miner who, with his blankets on his back, came strolling that way."

Gertrude Atherton (1857–1948)
The Mouth that Roared

Miss Manners would never have approved. First budding novelist Gertrude (née Horn) Atherton eloped with her own mother's well-heeled fiancé. ("Oh, well, I don't care. One has to marry sometime, I suppose," yawned the naughty nineteen-year-old.) Then she whined that the upper-crust lifestyle in bucolic Menlo Park, California, mostly consisted of "sitting round on verandahs." Maternity, too, proved merely a fleeting distraction: After Atherton glued her toddler's protruding ears to his head, her mother-in-law deemed it best to oversee his care herself. And as for husband George, "I couldn't talk to him, for he was interested in nothing but horses."

Unfortunately for garrulous Gertie, inadequate conversational skills scarcely constituted reasonable grounds for divorce, nineteenth-century American style. Still, there were other techniques for disposing of an inconvenient spouse. Spiking George's cocktail with glass shards came to mind, as did pouring boiling lead into his ear. So, regrettably, did the fact that there were "no private baths in jails." Fortunately for the sake of personal hygiene, Atherton's not-so-dearly beloved finally returned from a tragic sea voyage in 1887 preserved in a keg of rum. Quoth the greatly relieved bereaved: "Always nebulous, he had receded into the ether of which he had been born."

Given her druthers, Atherton would likewise have receded—not into the ether, but into ancient Egypt, where (or so she constantly commented) a race of powerhouse Amazons lorded it over their docile, ultra-domesticated spouses. Time travel not being among her talents, however, she contented herself with a lifelong orgy of globe-trotting and writing, spewing forth a book a year during her half-century of unwedded bliss. Apparently mindful of the motto "Write about what you know," the acid-tongued author proved quite partial to homicidal heroines and gentlemen who met untimely ends. But her venom was more versatile than that: Former friends were not amused to crack the cover of the roman à clef titled *A Daughter of the Vine*, only to have the skeletons (not to mention the bottles) in their closets come tumbling out. Perhaps because the subject was already deceased, however, Atherton's rigorously researched treatment of the life of Alexander Hamilton offended no one: *The Conqueror* sold nearly a million copies and introduced American bibliophiles to the biographical novel.

Even a type A career gal, however, requires a bit of diversion from time to time: During the odd leisure moment, Atherton particularly enjoyed toying with the affections of smitten suitors. "It is one thing to enjoy a man's society for an hour or two now and then, and another to annex him permanently," she shrugged. Nor did the outrage of her victims—whether of the literary or libidinous variety—unduly fret the wicked widow. "The worst trial I had...to endure," she revealed in her autobiography, "was having a husband continually on my hands."

Ann Eliza Young (1844–1908)
Heretic in the Harem

Brigham Young's twenty-four-year-old bride was scarcely ignorant
of the facts of Salt Lake City life when she tied a rather frayed knot
(her second, his twenty-seventh) with the polygamous Mormon
powermeister in 1869. "Most Mormon men discuss women with
reference to their 'points,' as jockeys would talk of horses," Ann Eliza
Young acknowledged in her autobiography. On the other hand, her
sixty-eight-year-old spouse was rumored to be worth a cool eight
million dollars. Under the circumstances, the young wife (who had
two tiny sons to support) didn't much mind if the geriatric groom was
a born-again male chauvinist pig, just so long as he came through
with the cash.

But alas, the president of the Church of Jesus Christ of Latter-Day
Saints proved to be a complete bust as a meal ticket. Only winsome
wife twenty-five, the apple of Brigham's eye, feasted on strawberries
and squab; for less significant spouses, staple fare at the vast
communal table consisted of little more than bread and dried-peach
sauce. The miserly Mormon doled out sundries with a frugal hand,
allotting each loved one no more than a solitary bar of soap each
month. When the twenty-seventh Mrs. Young hinted hopefully for
furs, her husband demanded to know if she thought money grew on
cactus plants. And even a private residence of her own ("Such a home
it was!") failed to pacify: The "dreaded monster" had outfitted it with

cheap pine furniture and chipped secondhand china. The final straw snapped—just four years into the theoretically eternal union—when the embittered bride begged her one-and-only to replace her defective cookstove. "Get it yourself," snarled the vice-regent of Christ on Earth.

Within the week, Mrs. Young served the penny-pinching prophet with a petition for divorce on the grounds of neglect and nonsupport, and act of defiance that earned her not only the permanent contempt of the Salt Lake community, but the avid attention of voyeuristic Victorians across the nation. Even at the expense of great personal revulsion, it seemed, morally minded non-Mormons felt compelled to learn all about the shocking sex lives of the Latter-Day Saints. Soon the self-styled "Rebel of the Harem" was racking up a respectable fortune of her own, lecturing coast to coast on titillating topics such as "Life in Mormon Bondage" and "Polygamy as It Is."

According to the Saintly school of spirituality, however, the erstwhile Mrs. Young was the only sinner in the post-marital scenario, a heretical harridan who had just purchased herself a one-way ticket to the underworld. But flush with fame and financial success, and no longer shivering in the chill sunshine of Brigham's love, the professional ex-wife evidently didn't give a hoot about the hereafter. At least the firewood wasn't rationed in hell.

> "The only good counsel I ever received from him
> was to practice the strictest economy."
>
> —A. E. Y.

TWISTED SISTERS AND MORTIFYING MOTHERS

Sarah Yates (1822–1892) and Adelaide Yates (1823–1917)

The Ties that Bind

History, with her usual insouciant disregard for the truly important details, offers no clue as to who caught the bouquet. But when teenage sisters Adelaide and Sarah Yates met twin brothers Chang and Eng Bunker at the wedding of mutual friends in 1838, sparks flew in multiple directions. And indeed, why shouldn't two of the most eligible bachelorettes in Wilkes County, North Carolina, engage in a pleasant flirtation with a pair of dark, handsome strangers? As it happened, many a glowering guest could think of a number of reasons—first and foremost, the fact that Chang and Eng, the famous original Siamese twins, were bound permanently at mid-chest by a flexible five-inch ligament.

It was, after all, an era when God-fearing women felt obliged to bathe in their nightgowns, lest they be somehow offended by the sight of their own naked bodies. Naturally, no virtuous young lady would consider the prospect of matrimony (and all that it implied) with a man so literally attached to his brother. "What a pity that you who love ladies so dearly can't marry, and that two young ladies can't have such lovely husbands as you would have been," sighed Adelaide. "Goodbye," remarked Sarah (who was keeping company with a parson), somewhat less wistfully.

Taking these comments as a sign of encouragement, the Bunker brothers pressed their mutual suit. As veterans of numerous P. T. Barnum exhibition tours, they knew exactly how to work their audience. There were flute serenades. There were charming declarations of love. There were cozy dinners chez Yates, where the brothers won the heart of Mother Yates, a five-hundred-pound beauty well acquainted with variations on the classic body shape.

In the end, Adelaide gave Chang to understand that his passion was not unrequited. Sarah, for her part, turned a perversely deaf ear toward Eng's entreaties until her sister appealed to her altruism. Why should she, Adelaide, suffer the ignominy of a ménage à trois instead of enjoying the comparative decorum of a face-saving four-way marriage? All Sarah had to do was say the word.

The Yates-Bunker nuptials in 1843 were followed by what one guest described as a "most elegant supper" and a gala cotillion that "set the Twins flying round with the ladies in the blissful delirium of the dance." With regard to other forms of blissful delirium, suffice it to say that during their thirty-one years of joint marriage, Sarah and Adelaide produced twenty-one children between them. As to the bedroom acrobatics involved, one can only speculate.

THE BRIDEGROOMS THEMSELVES: ENG AND CHANG

> "It is ridiculous to think you can spend your entire life with just one person. Three is about the right number."
>
> —Clare Boothe Luce

Mountain Mama

Mountaineer Fanny Workman didn't allow maternity to put a crimp in her crampons. Depositing daughter Rachel in a British boarding school, she set off in the mid-1890s to cycle through Java and Algeria, huff and puff her way across the Himalayas, and assail the twenty-thousand-foot crest of Mt. Koser Gunga—an accomplishment that earned her the women's altitude record in 1903. Not once, however, did the peripatetic parent mention her daughter in any of her nine travel books or offer to include her in any lofty adventures. As peak experiences went, motherhood evidently just didn't make the grade.

Belle Starr (1848–1889)
Mama Tried

According to one jaded judge, the infamous Belle Starr possessed "all the accomplishments of the highwayman." And indeed, few who did business with the brazen bandit—variously a road agent, cattle rustler, and head honcho of a gang of horse thieves—were inclined to argue the point. But evidently there was more to Ms. Starr than met the eye. In addition to her well-known feats of machismo, "The Petticoat Terror of the Plains" boasted a number of maternal achievements as well.

True, the bacon that breadwinner Belle (who outlived four outlaw husbands in a row) fried up was usually of the boosted breed. Well aware that her progeny shouldn't live on stolen swine alone, however, the pistol-packing parent plied little Edward and Pearl with generous helpings of culture. a library of leather-bound books and a decidedly upright piano graced the living room in Younger's Bend, Starr's cozy Arkansas hideaway for lawbreakers on the lam. At Belle's behest, Pearl suffered through a series of dance lessons, though her tendency to swoon on stage soon convinced Mamma that her daughter wasn't destined to become a prima donna. And naturally Starr tried to shield the children from her criminal connections, passing off, for example, the visiting Jesse James as "one Mr. Williams from Texas."

In 1883, however, a conviction on charges of horse theft compelled Starr to explain to her offspring—as sweetly as she could—the facts of outlaw life. "Now, Pearl, there is a vast difference in that place and a penitentiary," she wrote, after being sentenced to a nine-month stint in the Detroit House of Corrections. "You must bear that in mind and not think of mamma being shut up in a gloomy prison. It is said to be one of the finest institutions in the United States, surrounded by beautiful grounds, with fountains and everything nice."

Mother-daughter relations, however, grew somewhat strained after Starr's release from that most refined of all reformatories. Resuming her domestic duties with customary vigor, she launched an all-out search for a suitable spouse for Pearl, the ideal candidate being what she referred to as a "$25,000 man." Unbeknownst to the maternal matchmaker, however, her pride-and-joy had already pledged her troth to a youth whose assets were in no way financial, and Starr—six-shooters blazing—took it upon herself to chase him out of the county.

In the end, sad to say, Pearl wound up neither a ballerina nor a rich man's bride, but the proprietor of a popular brothel. Edward, for his part, evolved into a boozy lowlife, destined to perish in a saloon brawl in 1896. But their mother never had the luxury of wondering where she went wrong; she died two days before her forty-first birthday, shot in the back by an unknown assailant. Still, her performance as a parent wasn't entirely deserving of reproach. Mindful of the manners Mamma had taught her, Pearl managed to pen the *nicest* little epitaph, and she had it engraved on Belle's tomb at Younger's Bend:

Shed not for her the bitter tear
Nor give the heart to vain regret
'Tis but the casket that lies here
The gem that filled it sparkles yet.

—P. S.

Margaret Fox (1836–1893) and Kate Fox (1839–1892)
Material Girls

On March 31, 1848, Margaret Fox (twelve) and her sister Kate (nine) revealed to their proud parents that otherworldly spirits were trying to communicate with them. What else, after all, could account for the mysterious rapping sounds ricocheting through their home in Hydesville, New York? Soon the two sisters had worked out the supernatural Morse code to their satisfaction and were treating the provincial local populace to gratis translations of messages from the beyond.

Rather less baffling than the rapping, however, was Mama's motive for hauling the girls off to New York City in 1850, where she charged all comers a fee of one dollar for the privilege of seancing with her daughters. Oddly enough, such worldly visitors as Jenny Lind (who received her esoteric communiques in Swedish) and Horace Greeley (who did not) utterly failed to pick up on the materialistic vibrations hovering in the room. They were, however, impressed by the apparition of Benjamin Franklin, who obligingly struck a match so everyone could get a better look at him.

The fame (and not incidentally, the fortune) of the Foxes grew rapidly, especially with the endorsements of prominent personages such as

Greeley (who declared himself "convinced beyond a doubt of their perfect integrity and good faith"), First Lady Jane Pierce, and the governor of Wisconsin, who found the divining duo indispensable in his efforts to communicate with John C. Calhoun. Adding poltergeism and automatic writing to their psychic repertoire, the eerie sisters were to reign for four full decades as the preeminent occultists of the nation. (Particularly lucrative were the Civil War years, when bereaved wives and mothers gladly paid top dollar to contact patriots who had passed on.)

Even true believers, however, found it difficult to sustain their faith when in 1888, Margaret, now fifty-two, made a shocking confession: "Spiritualism," she announced to an astonished audience at New York's Academy of Music, "is a fraud." Not once in her life, she revealed, had she ever performed a genuine psychic feat. True, she had given it her best shot, even haunting cemeteries in the dead of night in the hopes of striking up some sort of ectoplasmic conversation. But sorry to say, not one corpse had ever responded to her attempts to communicate. Following a lengthy apology, the humbled hoaxtress wandered barefoot into the audience, placed her foot on the instep of a startled gentleman, and demonstrated how she made the rapping sounds with her big toe.

Margaret never did divulge the technique (whether anatomical or technological) which had allowed her to conjure up Mr. Franklin; presumably the explanation was equally innocuous. Nonetheless, the fraudulent Foxes had in their own misguided way accomplished something of note. In an era when children were supposed to be seen and not heard, it wasn't every young girl who could get a rise out of the entire nation just by cracking her toes.

"I was too honest to remain a medium."

—M. F.

Surprise Fighter

Hessie Donahue wasn't the kind of woman to pull any punches. During an 1892 all-comers boxing exhibition in Arkansas, she climbed into the ring with world-renowned champion John L. Sullivan and promptly knocked him out cold. It is not known whether this blow to Mr. Sullivan's self-esteem contributed in any way to his loss later that year to Gentleman Jim Corbett.

Eleanor Brittain (1834–1907)
A Grueling Ordeal

By the age of thirty-five, homesteader Eleanor Brittain recorded in her diary, she had crossed the plains in a covered wagon, survived the protracted illness and death of her husband, and was successfully supporting her three children as a schoolteacher. Protecting her eldest daughter's chastity from the predatory men of the notorious Gruwell clan, however, was one challenge that nearly drove the spunky single mama to despair.

Regrettably, no clue remains as to whether the Gruwells (who presented their loathsome visages on practically every page of Brittain's journal) constituted a general threat to teenage virtue in Northern California, or whether they had simply singled out young Helene—just fifteen and fresh of face—as a particularly hot prospect. In any event, Brittain reported, the situation was so serious that her ill-fated spouse had warned her with his dying breath to always "beware of the Gruwells."

Unfortunately, however, those pesky Gruwells kept turning up like cooties in a flour barrel. "My school is nice, and everything is all right," Brittain wrote in April 1870. However, she added, a friend had spotted Helene "in company with a Gentleman in Calistoga, and from the discription [sic] he gave, I new [sic] it was a Gruwell." Losing no time, Brittain hopped a stage and retrieved the hapless Helene, who like the reader, may or may not have known precisely what kind of danger she was courting. "Everything was all right then," Brittain concluded.

But in September, a Gruwell (whether late of Calistoga or an entirely different member of that ubiquitous family is not entirely clear) was back, driving up bold as brass in his buggy to collect the fair fifteen-year-old. "I stopped him," wrote Brittain, "and said Mr. Sam Gruwell, what do you want." Nothing but a drink of water, smirked that crafty cradle robber, who persisted in denying his dishonorable intentions. "He told me...that he did not want her nor none of her family," raged Helene's apoplectic parent, who like most mothers, simply couldn't stand being lied to. "His whip was standing in the Buggy. I taken it and gave him Two keen cuts with it and told him I would whip him untill [sic] he acknowledged what he wanted." And thus was routed the gruesome specter of Gruwell, who (or so the maternal guardian of maidenhood reported with great satisfaction) "drove away in a hurry," presumably never to return.

> "I don't know why a man wants to marry
> a girl not sixteen years old."
>
> —E. B.

Spokeswoman

Her family would have preferred that she travel in tandem—or better yet, not at all. But Miss Margaret Le Long of Chicago thought she looked perfectly sweet upon the seat of a bicycle built for one. In 1896, encumbered only by a change of underwear and a pistol, she mounted her trusty two-wheeler and pedaled off into the sunset, with San Francisco as her stated destination. Arriving safe and sound some two months later, Le Long reported that nobody had given her the least bit of trouble during her trip, probably because she wore a dress and not "unladylike bloomers." She did, however, note that her heater had come in handy in Wyoming when she had to break up a lethargic herd of cattle.

MAIDENS À LA MODE

Amelia Bloomer (1818–1894)
A Late Bloomer

Feminist Amelia Bloomer never intended to start a fashion revolution. As editor and owner of *The Lily*, the first American women's journal actually produced by a woman, the Seneca Falls suffragist was more concerned with politics than petticoats. But in 1850, the contents of her closet (not to mention those of *The Lily*) underwent one of the most publicized overhauls in history, thanks to the influence of one Elizabeth Miller.

It seems that Miller (cousin to Elizabeth Cady Stanton) breezed into town one day sporting Turkish trousers and a tunic of her own design. In an era when even the most delicate damsel carried fifteen or so pounds of clothing on her fragile form, Miller's lightweight ensemble packed quite a symbolic punch. Boldly, Bloomer cast off her own shackles and exhorted her readers to follow suit. "Fit yourself for a higher sphere and cease groveling in the dirt," she urged; "Let there be no stain of earth upon your soul or your apparel." Soon *The Lily*'s mailbox overflowed with letters requesting patterns for the comfortable new costume—as well as on occasion tips for appropriate accessorization.

Not everyone, however, embraced Bloomer's vision of a nation of stripped-for-action females. "The Bible is against bloomers," cried one moralistic matron, pointing out a passage in Deuteronomy which inveighed against women wearing "inexpressibles" (as semantically sensitive Victorians so blushingly termed their trousers). "We believe in the petticoat as an institution older and more sacred than the

Magna Carta," proclaimed *Harper's* magazine in 1857. Even Elizabeth Cady Stanton's supportive spouse expressed some anxiety concerning the propriety of the ensemble. "Ladies will expose their legs somewhat above the knee," he worried, "to the delight of those gentlemen who are anxious to know whether their lady friends have round and plump legs, or lean and scrawny ones."

Thanks to the fashion-conscious controversy, however, Bloomer's career as a women's rights lecturer flourished and she drew capacity crowds up and down the Eastern Seaboard. As to whether her audiences were more interested in analyzing her views or viewing her anatomy, the pragmatic publisher wasn't overly concerned. "If the dress drew the crowds that came to hear me, it was well," she explained; "They heard the message I brought them."

BLOOMING ETERNAL

"In the minds of some people the short dress and women's rights were inseparably connected."

—A. B.

Elsa Jane Guerin, a.k.a. "Mountain Charley" (1837-?)

Yen for Yang

Long before slinky stars Lady Gaga and Katy Perry were even twinkles in their mamas' eyes, nothing came between erstwhile Southern belle Elsa Jane Guerin and her dudely duds. Making a cross-dressing fashion statement, however, was the last thing on sixteen-year-old Guerin's mind in 1853 when she slipped into her first pair of trousers. Preposterously prematurely made a widow with two young daughters to support, her sole goal was to increase her earning potential. "I knew how great are the prejudices to be overcome by any young woman who seeks to earn an honest livelihood," she would later explain in her memoirs.

As a swaggering, gravel-voiced incarnation of machismo, Guerin quickly landed a lucrative position as "cabin boy" on a Mississippi steamer. Just as swiftly, she took to both the fiscal and physical benefits of manhood. Soon, the newly minted male wrote, she had begun "to rather like the freedom of my new character." Sans the symbolic shackles of petticoats, "I could go where I chose, do many things...debarred by propriety from association with the female sex." For the sake of her children, Guerin tried time and again to resume the costume of a more conventional mama. But in the end, her babies bored her, and as she was "unable to wholly eradicate many of the tastes which I had acquired during my life as one of the stronger sex," she gave herself over to her male persona.

Leaving behind both her children and a first name that no longer fit, Guerin restyled herself as "Mountain Charley" and headed for the wide-open West "determined to seek adventure in some new direction." Or perhaps *every* new direction: Guerin's very virile occupations over the years would include those of wagon train driver, railroad brakeman, gold miner, fur trader, and proprietor of a Denver saloon named after herself. On a more conventional note, her resume also eventually included another shot at the role of wife. To the end of her days, however, Guerin continued to gambol about in male garb. Only her second husband, Mr. Mountain Charley, was on occasion permitted to separate his wife from her studly threads.

> "I buried my sex in my heart and roughened the surface so that the grave would not be discovered."
> —E. J. G.

An Undercover Affair

In 1895, cross-dressing wasn't yet an integral part of the San Francisco social scene. Hence the valiant efforts of Mr. Milton Matson (a.k.a. Luisa Matson), an employee of the San Francisco Public Library, to keep her true identity hush-hush. Another good reason was Matson's fiancée, a local schoolteacher who was not, alas, even slightly amused to find she had inadvertently pledged her troth to a gal.

Dressed for Disaster

It was no accident that cute candy-stripers were few and far between in the Union Army Nursing Corps. Would-be bandage wrappers didn't get the nod from superintendent Dorothea Dix unless they were plain, proper, and post thirty. "Their dresses must be brown or black," dictated dour Dorothea; curls, bangles, and bows were also strictly verboten. War isn't pretty, and—strictly for the good of the troops, of course—neither were Dix's ladies.

Babe Bean (circa 1870–1936)
Not Suited for Sin

Girls who grow up among nuns can't help forming some peculiar ideas about fashion do's and don'ts. Few, however, emerge as full-fledged cross-dressers. Not so rebel-without-a-corset Babe Bean, whose unconventional mode of attire engendered a coast-to-coast controversy in the late 1890s.

A stint as a wimple-wearer was *supposed* to make a lady out of the tomboyish preteen, who actually entered the world as Elvira Virginia Mugarrieta—or so her etiquette-conscious parents (Mr. Mugarrieta founded the Mexican consulate in San Francisco) erroneously believed. Chafing under her crucifix, however, Bean longed not for lacy lingerie or love letters, but simply, as she later recalled, for "the liberty that the world sees fit to allow a boy."

At fifteen, she escaped the confines of the convent by marrying her brother's best friend, whom she promptly divorced. His sartorial style, however, turned out to be a keeper. "As a man," she wrote, "I can travel freely, feel protected, and find work." After a few years on the road, the religious refugee settled down on a houseboat on Lake McLeod, just outside Stockton, California. Her peculiar address, however, didn't interest vigilant local gendarmes nearly so much as her natty ensemble, which consisted of a blue pantsuit, white silk shirt, and rakishly angled fedora. In 1897, she was apprehended for the very nineteenth-century misdemeanor of "masquerading in men's clothing."

Soon thereafter, the "Trousered Puzzle," as one newspaper dubbed Bean, blossomed into a one-woman national media phenomenon. Scarcely a week passed during which her most mundane activities weren't written up on one front page or another. The local Bachelor's Club made her an honorary member, and the *Stockton Evening Mail* hired her as a celebrity reporter. Only the blockbuster headlines of the Spanish-American War in 1898, in fact, would finally knock her out of the news.

In the interim, however, numerous ladies (whose stays were perhaps too tightly laced to allow a healthy flow of blood to the brain) found freewheeling Bean a bitter pill to swallow. "There used to be a law against females dressing like the male human being," sniffed a letter to the *Evening Mail* signed by "The Girls of Stockton." "Some fine evening, there are going to be about twenty-five young women...all dressed in men's clothing, and we're going to go to the ark and get Babe Bean and duck her in McLeod's Lake till she cries, 'Nuff.' "

But the famous fashion victim, who lived modestly as a church mouse and had never sought the limelight in the first place, merely turned the other cheek—though not, it appears, without first inserting her rather tart tongue. "I wish to state that boys' clothes are still selling in Stockton at reduced prices," she responded, summoning up precisely the amount of Christian charity the circumstances required; "You are quite welcome to that information.

"It is your privilege to dress as you see fit, whether it is after the fashion of Venus or after the fashion of Babe Bean."

—B. B.

Mary Walker (1832–1919)
Dress Blues

In 1848, Mary Walker's father, a progressive New York physician, took his daughter aside for a candid chat about corsets. Terming those stylish undergarments "steel torture instruments," he extracted the solemn promise of the sixteen-year-old surgeon-to-be that she would never become a bimbo in whalebone. As it turned out, Dad needn't have bothered: Blessed with petite proportions and massive ambitions, Walker, who took her degree from Syracuse Medical College in 1855, was far more interested in carving out a career for herself than whittling her waist.

Apparently she wielded a scalpel with skill, for in 1864, the Union Army officially commissioned Walker as an assistant surgeon, her corsetless condition notwithstanding. But even with the country going to hell in a handbag, conventions in couture did not follow suit so swiftly, and only a special act of Congress allowed Walker to adopt the official dark-blue trousers and tunic befitting her rank as first lieutenant. Thus liberated from ladies' wear, the mobile MD proceeded to transgress other traditional boundaries at will—in 1864, she was captured by Confederate soldiers when she crossed enemy lines to treat civilians. For the Union, the incident constituted no more than a minor blow; but for nineteenth-century feminism, it was to prove an unprecedented triumph. After four months in captivity, the cross-dressing doctor was exchanged for a male prisoner of equal rank—one of the first instances in military history when a woman's worth was deemed equivalent to that of a man.

Postwar, the patriotic physician promptly shed her dress blues, though evidently not her distaste for dresses. Now turned out in a frock coat and striped trousers, Walker took to the lectern to argue against a womanly wardrobe as unhealthy, aesthetically displeasing, and on occasion, downright dangerous. Not that female fashion victims bore sole responsibility for their folly: "If men were really what they profess to be," she suggested, "they would not compel women to dress so that the facilities for vice would always be so easy." In an abundance of caution, the sartorial strategist sometimes even beefed up security on her trousers by draping an American flag across her lap.

As Walker was well aware, however, it was only in the most superficial sense that she could take refuge beneath the Stars and Stripes. "Any law of the State which...denies [women] any privileges enjoyed by men is hereby declared to be in conflict with the Constitution of the United States," read the feisty physician's *Crowning Constitutional Argument*, an ahead-of-its-time equal rights amendment drafted in her eightieth year as a voteless Victorian. Unfortunately, the *"Crowing" Argument* (as one government scribe managed, in most Freudian fashion, to mistranscribe the title) never saw the light of day. Like Walker's well-intentioned papa, Uncle Same might occasionally grant his nieces permission to dress in masculine mode, should they so desire. but the rights and privileges pertaining thereto, it seemed, they would simply have to seize for themselves.

THE DIMINUTIVE DOCTOR

"The greatest sorrows from which women suffer to-day are...caused by their unhygienic manner of dressing. The want of the ballot is but a toy in comparison!"

—M. W.

HATCHET QUEENS AND PISTOL PACKERS

Carrie Nation (1846–1911)
Battle Ax

Okay, so the mother of legendary temperance crusader Carrie Nation wasn't *really* Queen Victoria. It was just Mom's syphilis-induced delusions, it seems, that prompted her to parade about in purple velvet, sporting a curious little crystal crown. Nonetheless, nineteen-year-old Nation's reaction to her first kiss was a classic in the Victorian nice-girls-don't genre: "I am ruined! I am ruined!" bellowed the 180-pound innocent, flinging her meaty arms in the air in a great display of maidenly distress.

That coy declaration, however, marked the end of Nation's career as a shrinking violet. Though the caddish osculator eventually won her heart, she never forgave him for showing up pickled to the gills on their wedding day in 1867—nor for promptly drinking himself into an early grave. "I did not find [him] the lover I expected," she tattled. And a decade later, husband number two—a teetotaling Kansas minister—proved such a disappointment that Nation frequently found it necessary to rise in church and rebuke him.

Of course, that was after angelic voices had revealed Nation's true mission in life: to personally vanquish every social vice that inspired her wrath. Thus divinely inspired, Nation soon set about making every man on earth—or at least in her immediate vicinity—as miserable as humanly possible. "I have the right to take cigars and cigarettes from men's mouths in self-defense," she noted, and acted accordingly.

Men's clubs also rankled deep in her heart, and she startled many a passing stranger by ripping the Masonic Order pin from his lapel.

It was in the gin mills of Kansas, however, that Nation's talent for ax grinding truly blossomed. Unlike the lush who exits the barroom on his knees, Nation actually *entered* that way—praying, weeping, belting out hymns, and doing her damnedest to disturb the peace. Next came missile warfare. "I smashed five saloons with rocks," she once bragged; "God was certainly standing by me." (Or more likely, just behind her, safely out of harm's way.)

Ultimately, however, it was a practice she liked to call the "hatchetation of joints" that proved the most deadly weapon in Nation's arsenal of ball-breaking strategies. "I am going to break this place up," she would calmly announce to the barkeep. Before startled patrons could stir from their stools, the hatchet-happy harpy would whirl into action, shattering mirrors, smashing bottles and glasses to the ground, and savagely hacking away at those beloved barroom paintings depicting buxom young ladies in various states of undress.

In the final analysis, Nation's angelically inspired antics clearly paved the way for sweeping temperance reforms from coast to coast. But in her autobiography, the crackpot crusader revealed more than she probably intended about the genuine source of her saloon-smashing passion: "I loved him more than my own life," she sighed, waxing wistful about her original soused spouse; "But [he] seemed to want to be away from me."

"Men are nicotine-soaked, beer-besmirched, whiskey-greased, red-eyed devils."

—C. N.

Martha Maxwell (1831–1881)
Notorious Naturalist

No-one ever accused eagle-eyed Martha Maxwell of possessing the grace of a gazelle or the innocent gaze of a fawn. On occasion, however, the foremost female naturalist of nineteenth-century America did catch some heat for blowing away more than her fair share of Bambis. To Maxwell, human flesh was sacrosanct: "How could you do it!" she scolded a daughter who dared to pierce her ears; "It is a relic of barbarism." But when it came to her favorite fauna finds, the hard-boiled Colorado huntress shrank neither from shooting them nor preserving them for posterity via the macabre art of taxidermy.

In her defense, Maxwell could only plead that she didn't kill in cold blood. At the tender age of ten, the budding rifle queen of the Rockies had nailed a rattler, thereby saving the life of her little sister. By age twenty-nine, however, her aim was primarily to "immortalize" the furry friends she encountered on solo camping expeditions in the remote Rocky Mountain wilderness. (Permanently *immobilizing* those captivating creatures, it seems, was merely a regrettable side effect.)

By all accounts, Maxwell's dazzling diorama of moribund mammals (housed, oddly enough, in a building devoted to "Women's Work") was one of the killer attractions of the 1876 Centennial Exhibit in Philadelphia. "I don't believe them critters was shot," exclaimed one visitor, examining at close range the doughty deerslayer's handiwork. "I've looked 'em all over, and I can't see any holes."

Some detractors, however, thought they detected lamentable lacunae in Maxwell's moral development. As her sister was heard to sigh, "The sight of a new specimen always affected her, as the smell of alcohol is said to affect an inebriate." But the ardent animal lover refused to accept criticism from any save the certifiably noncarnivorous. "There isn't a day you don't tacitly consent to have some creature killed so you may eat it," she retorted. According to her, it was a far, far nobler thing to stuff one's prey than one's face.

> "I leave it to you. Which is more cruel? To
> kill to eat or to kill to immortalize?"
>
> —M. M.

The Macabre Medium

Just as Kansas occultist Katie Bender claimed, she could indeed cure "Fits, Deafness and all such diseases." Regrettably, however, Ms. Bender's promotional materials failed to mention certain unpleasant side effects of her peculiar panacea. In 1874, local authorities unearthed eight decidedly unfitful corpses in her garden, all victims of the psychotic psychic's sledgehammer.

Dating Herself

Perhaps the virtue of *some* working girls was so relaxed as to border on the catatonic. But San Francisco shop clerk Lillian Blair, who sued the former President of Guatemala in 1897 for breach of proper dating protocol, was made of starchier stuff. El Presidente's official offense? "He took me to the Palace Hotel to dine in his private parlor and meet some of his friends, and introduced me to a number of Spanish gentlemen," revealed the puritanical plaintiff, who apparently did not care either for rich food or rich foreigners.

Lizzie Borden (1860–1927)
Hatchet-Job Heiress

In the storybook, sinless Cinderella languished like a lady, patiently waiting for some royal foot-fetishist to rescue her. But in 1892, flesh-and-blood Lizzie Borden of Fall River decided to deal with the wicked stepmother situation in a different way. Or so claimed the State of Massachusetts, which tried Borden in 1893 for the brutal bludgeoning of both her surrogate mama and doting papa.

According to the prosecution, the thirty-two-year-old Sunday school teacher was provoked to murderous passion by suspicions that her wealthy father, then seventy years of age, would leave all his loot to the loathsome second spouse. Foiled in her efforts to poison the pair with prussic acid, Borden instead executed the affair with an ax, then calmly burned her blood-spattered dress. The district attorney made a pointed inquiry: "Were you cordial with your stepmother?" But the demure defendant—who offered the alibi that she had been out searching for sighing sinkers at the time of the crime—was not to fall so easily into the Oedipal trap. "That depends," she hedged, "on one's idea of cordiality."

So far as the State of Massachusetts was concerned, however, addressing one's parents with an ax did not fall under the rubric of civilized domestic intercourse, and its curiosity about Borden's behavior on the fateful day proved insatiable. ("Did you see [your father's] eyeball hanging out?" it inquired with interest; "See the gashes where his face was laid open?" But Borden—bolstered by the sisterly support of prominent suffragists and the Women's Christian Temperance Union—denied all. Though circumstantial evidence did indeed point in her direction, the prosecution could produce no confession, no witnesses to the crimes, and no positively identifiable murder weapon. At the conclusion of the two-week trial, the jury deliberated only an hour before returning a not-guilty verdict.

Though Borden went to collect a $250,000 inheritance and purchase an opulent mansion in Fall River's finest neighborhood, she was never to recover from her fall from grace. Little inclined to bury the infamous hatchet, the community (and eventually, the nation) apparently found it more compelling to perpetuate the myth of the monstrous murderess. Nor did Borden's social standing soar when in 1904, she embarked upon a widely publicized affair with Nance O'Neill—an actress noted, interestingly enough, for imparting to the role of Lady Macbeth "a rage bordering on madness."

At least one resident, however, found a soft spot in his heart for the pariah who had put Fall River on the map. "She made a big hit with me by being my best customer when I had a lemonade stand," recalled former neighbor Russell Lake, who had known the aging outcast when he was a boy. But his juvenile character endorsement was not sufficient to cast doubt on Borden's authorship of the bloody deed, by now permanently inscribed in the popular imagination. What, after all, do innocent children know about original sin?

> Lizzie Borden took an ax
> And gave her mother forty whacks.
> When she saw what she had done
> She gave her father forty-one.
> —Anonymous

Agnes Morley Cleaveland (1874–1958)
Lariats of Fire

Quite frankly, Ada Morley didn't give a hoot if her daughter Agnes grew up to be a cowboy. Mrs. Morley had never really cottoned to life on her husband's isolated New Mexico ranch anyway. When he walked out on the family in the mid-1880s, she quickly delegated all the down-and-dirty details of managing the spread to barely adolescent Agnes and baby brother Ray. Contemplating great issues and corresponding with famous suffragists, it seems, were more Mom's cup of tea. ("What does Susan B. Anthony know about the cow business?" grumbled Ray.)

But while the lady of the house was pondering feminist ideology, her little girl was living it. sporting a five-gallon Stetson and denim knickers, Mademoiselle Morley worked the herds, tracked grizzlies, and fended off predators of every species. "Why are you not afraid?" wondered a swarthy horseman who overtook her as she was driving a supply wagon through desolate territory. In response, "I reached under the...seat and pulled out my little thirty-two," Morley recalled in *No Life for a Lady*, her aptly titled autobiography. Apparently this satisfied the gentleman's curiosity, for he rode off without posing any further questions. "We had a saying, 'A six-shooter makes all men equal,' " Morley wrote, "I amended it to, 'A six-shooter makes men and women equal.' " Even minus her firearms, however, young Morley was a dangerous dudette to cross, or so the local deputy sheriff discovered when he made the mistake of trying to repossess the petite cowpuncher's most prized pony. "Stop right where you are," Morley hissed, swinging a strap weighted with a heavy horse bell, "or I'll split your skull right open."

Defending the family homestead from a duo of marauding desperados one night, however, required a more sophisticated show of muscle. As Mom snoozed in the next room, Morley pumped up the charm, passed around a platter of sourdough doughnuts, and persuaded the bad-news boys to play a round of poker. (Naturally, she excelled at that manly art as well.) By daybreak, the yawning bandits, now twenty cents in the hole, were as subdued as Sunday morning. They meekly cooked breakfast, did the dishes, and departed professing great shame at having been "cleaned out by a girl."

Having conquered the frontier, Morley went on to captivate her classmates at sedate Stanford University—including mining student Newton Cleaveland, whom she married in 1899—with stories of her wild-and-woolly girlhood. But having heard so many of his bride's terrifying tales, Mr. Cleaveland was disinclined to relocate to nerve-wracking New Mexico, and Morley grudgingly conceded to settling in California. Settling *down*, however, was an entirely different matter. "That I myself have survived to a ripe maturity is due to great self-control in not having committed premeditated murder and been hanged," she mused thoughtfully, some fifty years later.

AGNES'S FAVORITE COMFORT ITEM

"A six-shooter does give one a sense of security."
—A. M. C.

The Killer Instinct

"Strapping young women" were welcome to give agriculturalist Augusta Main a hand with her harvest. But guys who knew what was good for them didn't trespass on the upstate New Yorker's turf. Arrested in 1897 for assaulting a male neighbor with murderous intent, Ms. Main confessed that she "never sees men or dogs but what [I] aches to kill them."

Annie Oakley, a.k.a. Phoebe Mozee (1860–1926)

Hired Gun

Even in the enlightened twentieth century, it's the rare matron who actually gets paid for taking potshots at her man. But for ace markswoman Annie Oakley, the shooting star of the Buffalo Bill Wild West Show from 1885 to 1901, firing a few bullets at husband Frank Butler was all in a day's work. The sharpshooter's spouse couldn't even savor a smoke onstage without having the smoldering cigarette shot right out of his mouth. When foolhardy Frank grasped a dime between thumb and forefinger, his wife got a kick out of blasting the coin from his grip. And should he feel compelled (for whatever obscure reason) to swing a weighted ball around his head, a savage spray of shot invariably threatened to rearrange the composition of his cranium.

Few Victorian gentlemen, of course, would have tolerated playing second fiddle on stage, let alone volunteered for such ammo-intensive abuse. But in 1875, at the age of fifteen, "the champion lady rifle shot of the world" had beaten the pants off her future partner at a Cincinnati shooting expedition. Fully aware he'd never repossess his trousers, Mr. Butler saw no reason why Oakley shouldn't simply continue to wear them after their marriage the following year.

Her mate was not alone, however, in rendering all due respect to a femme so potentially fatale. Chief Sitting Bull, for one, was utterly blown away by the trigger-happy thespian. As tokens of his esteem, the smitten Sioux gifted her with a golden nugget and a picture of himself and adopted her as his spiritual daughter in an official tribal ceremony. The King of Senegal, another acquisitive admirer, engaged in some rather abbreviated negotiations with Buffalo Bill regarding the asking price for a sure-shot "slave." His Majesty's fiefdom, it evolved, was overrun just then with man-eating tigers; he was willing to pay top dollar for a woman who knew her weapons. And late in the nineteenth century, the captivated Kaiser Wilhelm of Germany prevailed upon Oakley to extinguish his blazing butts in her own inimitable fashion. (In the light of subsequent historical events, it turned out, she was to regret the accuracy of her aim. But alas, the mad warmonger did not respond to her letter requesting a repeat of the stunt.)

It was Queen Victoria, however, who paid Oakley what she considered the "highest compliment." Following a command performance of the Wild West Show in London in 1887, the doughty dowager gave "a queer little nod of her head" and summoned the twenty-seven-year-old celebrity to her side. "You are a very, very clever little girl," she simpered. But Oakley needed no royal reminder that she had hit on a cushy career indeed. "Being just little Annie Oakley with ten minutes work once or twice a day was good enough for me, for I had...my freedom," she would later write. Needless to say, the genius gunslinger was careful never to jeopardize her enviable job by actually harming one precious hair on her husband's head.

> "A crowned queen was never treated by her courtiers with more reverence than I."
>
> —A. O.

DREADED DESPERADOS AND GUTSY GAMBLERS

Martha Jane Cannary, a.k.a. "Calamity Jane" (1852–1903)
She Slept Here...and There

No one knows precisely why Martha Jane Cannary—a booze-swilling, street-brawling, national disaster area of a woman—was dubbed "Calamity Jane." Gentlemen who acquired one of love's annoying little afflictions during a tryst with the Wild West's most willing sweetheart held one theory. "Darling Bob" Mackay, who wound up ducking bullets in a Dodge City dive due to an ill-considered remark regarding her lingerie, had his own explanation. And doubtless Jane's dozen-or-so main squeezes ("sometimes miscalled husbands," smirked one twentieth-century historian) who met violent ends could have provided other interesting insights.

In any event, the epithet clearly wasn't intended to flatter. But self-mythologizing Ms. Cannary, orphaned at fourteen and accustomed to scraping by however she could (over the years, her various real or perceived occupations included muleskinner, US Army scout, wagon freighter, and Indian fighter), didn't mind. In fact, with a street urchin's instinct for self-promotion, she did her best to live up to her notorious nickname.

"I'm Calamity Jane, and this drink's on the house," she thundered to Wyoming barkeeps. She laughed off any and all attempts at reform: "Aw, you go to hell, Hank. I don't take my preachin' from an old goat I've slept under the same blanket with more'n a hundred times."

She boasted that she had been banned from a brothel in Bozeman, Montana, as a bad influence on the B-girls. And, she bragged, she was the only woman in the West who had both worked the whorehouses and patronized them.

But if Jane's physique pertained to the public domain, her outlaw heart was the private property of glamorous Wild Bill Hickok. Regrettably, the formidably mustachioed frontiersman rode off into the sunset without returning her affections; he preferred, it seems, a more demure brand of feminine charm. Nonetheless, Jane (never a stickler for petty detail) named Hickok as the father of her daughter born in 1873, and thirty years later scored the ultimate coup by having herself buried next to him in a cemetery in Deadwood, South Dakota. "It's a good thing Bill is dead," remarked one of Mr. Hickok's cronies. "He'd never 'a stood for this."

Under the posthumous circumstances, however, the hapless Hickok— like every other man who tangled with the hell-raising harridan—had precious little say in the matter. As Jane herself once informed a startled stranger who found her snoozing off a private whiskey-fest in his living room: "I'm Calamity Jane, and I sleep when and where I damn please"—not to mention with whom.

SHE WANTED TO BE WILD BILL'S WOMAN

Jeanne 'Jenny' Bonnet (1849–1876)
Crimes of Compassion

Professional pickpocket and frog-catcher Jeanne Bonnet, who debuted as a child actress with the French Theatrical Troupe in San Francisco, could have had a fairy-tale career on the stage. "Had she but followed the course marked out for her, she would probably have become a bright ornament in the profession of her parents," lamented one journalist shortly after her demise, an event nearly as unladylike as it was untimely.

By the time she was fifteen, however, Bonnet was appearing in juvenile court rather than in juvenile parts and acting rather badly at the local reformatory. "Her ambition," it was reported, "was to become the Captain of a gang of robbers, which would terrorize the community as did the brigands in Sicily." Evidently the budding gangster did her best to dress the part: it was duly noted that she "discarded those garments which fashion has decreed should be worn by the gentler sex," and sported a jaunty man's hat "with all the grace of an experienced hoodlum." As the years went by, Bonnet's criminal caricatures grew ever more convincing; simply by eschewing female garb, she managed to rack up some twenty arrests for "wearing male attire."

Not until 1875, however, did the twenty-six-year-old offender launch her career as a labor organizer for lawbreakers. Those who euphemistically termed Bonnet a "man-hater" might have ascribed a different motive to her new habit of hanging out in whorehouses. But her intentions were pure: the plan, it seems, was to encourage her scarlet sisters to slip out from under the patriarchal thumb and into something more comfortable, i.e., the self-sufficient lifestyle of the petty larcenist. And indeed, ladies of the evening yearning to breathe free enthusiastically embraced the light-fingered way of life. Soon more politically correct miscreants were lifting wallets in San Francisco.

Parting the privileged from their cash, however, was a low-risk enterprise compared with liberating shady ladies from their procurers, few of whom were truly interested in feminist ideology—or so Bonnet learned, a tad too late, when she started keeping company with one of her protégées, a former fallen angel and circus rider by the name of Adele Beunon. Unfortunately, a certain gentleman of Ms. Beunon's acquaintance, accustomed to living off the wages of her sins, harbored a serious grudge against Bonnet for separating him from the source of his income. One dark September evening in 1876, as Bonnet lay waiting for Adele to join her in bed, a sniper's bullet flew through the window. She expired in her lover's arms, presumably the victim of a very perturbed pimp. Long before that tragic turn of events, of course, it was apparent that the deceased's brief life wasn't destined to go down in the happily-ever-after annals. But vigilant Victorian moralists managed to put a prim Brothers Grimm spin on the whole affair. Any heroine who kissed the princess instead of the frog, it was intimated, deserved exactly what she got.

"Whistling girls and crowing hens
always come to some bad end."
—Nineteenth century American proverb

Uncowed Courtesan

Among the numerous dubious accomplishments of Madam Pamela Mann were counterfeiting, forgery, and larceny. But that didn't mean she didn't know right from wrong. Having lent a yoke of oxen to General Sam Houston in 1836, Ms. Mann was not amused to discover that the fabled fighter had no intention of returning her property. "General, you told me a damn lie," she snapped when she finally caught up with him; "I want my oxen." And holding the toast of Texas at bay with "a pair of pistols and a long knife," the tough-talking trollop proceeded to liberate her livestock. To the great humiliation of the hapless hero, Mann's moral victory was ever after as "Houston's defeat."

Pearl Hart (1871-?)
The Prodigal Daughter

Contrary to cliché, not every hardened con was once some mother's beloved son. Even in the chivalrous late-nineteenth century, belles who failed to bow to convention were apt to wind up behind bars. Failure to faint on cue, after all, constituted a social misdemeanor, attiring oneself in trousers a legitimate legal offense. And as Canadian jailbird Pearl Hart discovered in 1899, even excessive filial devotion could land a lady in the big house.

Long before she committed her historic crime, however, Ms. Hart was eagerly experimenting with nontraditional ways of expressing her love; utterly indifferent to the fact that proper young ladies said, "I do" before they said, "You may," for example, she found herself a parent-to-be at the tender age of seventeen. Just because she had to get married, however, the affectionate Ontarian saw no reason to stay that way. Soon her husband was *histoire*; compared to the studly cowboys of Hart's prefeminist fantasies, a small-time gambler just didn't stand a chance.

Perhaps Hart's mother agreed that her charismatic child could do better for herself; in any event, she evidently didn't mind bringing up baby while her daughter headed south in pursuit of the American dream (preferably the sort sporting a Stetson). No doubt, however, Mom would have been reassured to know that the wanton wanderer never, ever, dispensed her favors for free. Cash on the barrelhead, as every boomtown boyfriend from Trinidad to Tucson knew, was Hart's MO, and cheapskates were apt to wake up with nasty headaches and empty pockets.

In an Arizona mining camp in 1899, Hart finally secured a suitably glamorous soul mate, a mustachioed miscreant by the manly name of Joe Boot. Having sworn eternal devotion, the starry-eyed pair went on to enjoy a successful dual mugging career: While one of the lovebirds would shove a gun in the victim's back, the other would relieve him of his wallet. Who knows what Boot did with his share of the take; Hart, for her part, mailed most of her loot home to Mama.

But the wages of small-scale sin simply couldn't cover the bills when Hart's mother fell victim to a serious (and seriously expensive) illness. Desperate times call for desperate measures: In Hart's professional opinion, only a stagecoach robbery could scare up the requisite cash. And indeed, planted square in the highway near Florence, Arizona, with "revolvers cocked and aim steady" (or so the wagon driver reported), Hart and Boot made quite a persuasive case for charitable donation, extracting a total of $431 from the three petrified passengers.

The law, however, found itself singularly unimpressed by this unique display of daughterly duty and sentenced the "famous lady highwayman" to five years at the all-male Territorial Prison at Yuma. "We'd better keep that woman far away from the other inmates," shuddered the warden's wife, who thought she knew a bad lot when she saw one; "She'll shock them with her language and corrupt their morals." Her fears, however, proved unfounded; there is absolutely no record of Hart attempting to tattoo the inscription *Mom* on either her own forearm or that of anyone else.

"Hands up!"

—P. H.

Mary Sawyer, a.k.a. Molly Monroe
(1847–1902)
A Dubious Dementia

No surviving records indicate why Mary Sawyer—a boisterous Arizona roustabout who dressed like a man, drank like a fish, and made the dry desert air crackle with her curses—was officially declared insane in 1877. Perhaps it was because Ms. Sawyer (otherwise known as Molly Monroe) bedded her beau without bothering to marry him, or even cleaning his house. Perhaps it was because she preferred grubbing for gold to embroidering tea towels. ("The 'boys' were out last week prospecting," reported the Prescott *Miner* in 1872; "George Monroe, Joe Fuggit, Wm. Gellaspie, Tom Graves, and Molly struck a galena lode.") Or perhaps it was because the hedonistic hoyden frankly reveled in the fact that she could "ride anything with four feet [and] chew more tobacco and swear harder than any man."

In any event, stints in various mental institutions of the West failed, utterly and spectacularly, to remold Sawyer into a more manageable format. Initially confined to a facility in Stockton, California, she was—as the *Miner* noted in 1877—transferred to San Quentin Prison after becoming "intent on burning the Asylum." And three years later, a Yuma journalist found her "entirely devoid of any higher aspirations than to go back and resume the wild and dissolute life she led in the mountains of Arizona." By the incorrigible inmate's own assessment, however, she suffered not from psychosis, but merely from pugnacity. Her sole affliction, she explained to her interviewer, was being "the meanest thing on earth," a condition that might be corrected were she only "turned out and allowed to do as she pleased."

Prison authorities, however, were not so easily persuaded to parole Sawyer. In 1895, she finally took matters into her own hands and made a break for freedom. Evidently nearly twenty years of incarceration had diminished neither her physical nor mental stamina, for the fiftyish fugitive eluded her pursuers for days, leading them on a wild foot-chase across the desert sands. "If I'd a' only had my breeches and my gun, I'd a' been all right," she muttered as she was finally recaptured—and she was probably correct.

But under the circumstances, Sawyer was not "all right": stripped of both trousers and dignity, she died in a Phoenix insane asylum in 1902. Even before her death, however, Arizona had set about prettifying the corpse of her memory, whittling a larger-than-life character down to a daintier size. According to the new, sanitized version of her story, Sawyer had been no wild-at-heart hellcat, but a "noble and charitable woman," tragically unhinged by some deep disappointment in love. Regrettably, it never seemed to occur to the mythologizing mop-up crew that her life needed no posthumous apologia. The day was yet to come, it appeared, when a woman who walked on the wild side might become a lovable legend rather than a lunatic.

"Sanity is a cozy lie."

—Susan Sontag

Story of a Sad Sack

In 1870, thirty-two-year-old Margaret Knight patented a product still in use today—the machine that produces square-bottomed paper bags. During the course of her career, the ingenious Massachusetts inventor would go on to claim credit for twenty-six other innovations, most of them in the field of heavy machinery. Regrettably, however, Knight's creativity did not extend to the realm of economics. She died with only $275 to her name, narrowly escaping becoming a bag lady of another sort entirely.

"Poker Alice" Tubbs (1851–1930)
Ace Accessorizer

"Poker Alice" Tubbs didn't have to read *Godey's Lady's Book* to know that accessories could really make or break an ensemble. For the gal who gambled, the classic deadpan look was always *en vogue*. Tubbs also understood intuitively that a Colt revolver made a snazzier sartorial accompaniment than a lace hankie—especially, it might be added, for the professional cardsharp who just happened to be a winsome blonde-haired, blue-eyed widow in her early twenties.

Not that Tubbs—a former Southern belle who was born in Britain and had the accent to prove it—ever engaged in much giddy girl talk about fashion do's and don'ts. For one thing, there were remarkably few females to chat up in the smokey saloons where she sat playing cards late into the night. For another, it wasn't all the easy to enunciate with her trademark cheroot smoldering between her lips. And finally, her garrulous gun—a constant companion on her peregrinations through the pleasure palaces of the Wild West—was a remarkably persuasive conversationalist in its own right.

Naturally, the chivalrous Colt spoke up for her when she caught a dirty dog dealing from the bottom of the deck in a Pecos, Texas, saloon. While the hot-tempered heater in her right hand addressed a few choice remarks to the shyster, Alice raked in the five-thousand-dollar kitty with her left and beat it out of town. Together, woman and weapon headed east for a week-long shopping spree in New York City, where five grand could still buy a decent set of duds and a gaudy bauble or two.

Then there was the little contretemps back in Deadwood, South Dakota, when a drunken prospector with a bowie knife took a notion to carve up boyfriend Bill (likewise a barfly bettor) like so many buffalo steaks. "Nothing doing," remarked Tubbs' revolver. "Let's get hitched," responded grateful Bill once the smoke had cleared. By 1893, the newly reformed lovebirds had settled down to an astonishingly virtuous life, adopting orphans (seven in all) and raising chickens on a small South Dakota homestead.

Domestic bliss, however, simply wasn't in the cards for Tubbs. After Bill's untimely death, the enterprising Missus transformed herself into a prosperous Madam in Sturgis, South Dakota. Naturally, the Colt came along for the ride. Inevitably, there arose a homicidal altercation between that feisty firearm and an obnoxious patron. (The resulting mess, incidentally, gave new meaning to the phrase *disorderly house*.) Oddly enough, however, the judge never got around to sending Tubbs—all tricked out in her Sunday best—to prison. It was, it seems, impossible to believe the demure femme fatale guilty of anything worse than harboring an accessory to the crime.

"I'd rather play poker with five or six experts than eat."

—A. T.

Eleanor Dumont, a.k.a. "Madame Moustache" (1829–1879)
Calculating Coquette

Like any down-and-dirty mining town, by the mid-1800s, Nevada City, California, had seen its share of fallen angels and good-time Gerties. Entirely without precedent, however, was elegant Eleanor Dumont, who stepped off the northbound stage one day in 1854, and within the week, was presiding over the most popular blackjack parlor in the county. No one ever knew precisely where the twenty-five-year-old Frenchwoman came from, or why. Even in nebulous Nevada City, however, everyone knew better than to call her "Madame Moustache," a sobriquet derived from a frankly luxuriant growth of lipline hair, to her face.

According to one biographer, Dumont's premier pleasure palace "was not only orderly beyond all local records—it trembled on the brink of becoming ill at ease." Rough-hewn roustabouts spit-shined muddy boots and ran a comb through matted locks in deference to the proprietress, obviously a gentlewoman born and bred. They sipped champagne instead of whiskey, smoked sparingly, and did their best to mute the more explosive ranges of their vocabularies. Most astonishing of all, such sacrifices were made toward the sole end of losing (as, in the end, everyone did) to a lady—albeit one with a thousand delightful ways of catering to the male ego. About herself, Dumont said little, which naturally rendered her all the more fascinating.

When the Nevada City boom went bust, the bonanza boys simply packed up their dreams and headed for the next Shangri-La on the horizon. So did Dumont, who was eventually to blaze a star-studded trail of elite resorts across the West. During her twenty-three years on the card-playing circuit, however, she remained an enigma, displaying to the world only the practiced charm crucial to her professional success.

But those who were present at her Bannock, Idaho, establishment on a certain night in 1864 caught a fleeting glimpse of the elusive *vingt-et-un* expert's true character. A rare fight had erupted, and Dumont's long-term lover (who doubled as her right-hand man at the gaming tables) took a fatal bullet. Under the circumstances, a touch of hysteria would surely not have been out of place. But Dumont merely had the corpse whisked out of sight, and—her face bland as a baguette—asked the murderer to fill in as her assistant. An alternative beau, it seemed, could be chosen at leisure, but the crowd of men waiting to be separated from their money required immediate attention.

Dumont disappeared from the western landscape as mysteriously as she had arrived; one morning in 1879, her lifeless body was discovered by the road two miles from Bodie, California, next to an empty bottle of poison. There was no note. Even in death, it seems, the secretive sophisticate played her cards close to the vest, deigning neither to apologize nor to explain.

"She was clever, and had a great deal of charm... I could never understand why she became a gambler."
—"Poker Alice" Tubbs on "Madame Moustache"

Gifted Gladiator

In 1876, Nell Saunders and Rose Harland of New York shared the honor of participating in the first public female boxing match in America. For her efforts, the victorious Miss Saunders received a lovely silver butter dish. Under the circumstances, perhaps a nice punch bowl would have been more appropriate.

GET IT?

Nellie Cashman (1854–?)

A Totally Excellent Babe

Perhaps because six-shooter sweethearts and pistol-happy prostitutes tended to attract more than their fair share of attention, it sometimes seems that the entire feminine population of the American frontier was comprised of reform school rejects. But as peripatetic prospector Nellie Cashman proved, it wasn't just bad girls who knew how to have a good time in the Wild West.

Known variously during her fifty-year career as the Frontier Angel, the Miner's Angel, and the Saint of the Sourdoughs, Cashman traipsed from Baja California to the Arctic Circle and back in her obsessive quest for ore, netting at least a half-dozen fortunes in the process. Sometimes—as in the case of a lucky $100,000 strike in the Alaska Territory—she sank her earnings right back into the ground. "What did I do with it?" she chortled; "I spent every red cent of it...prospecting the country. I went out with my dog team or on snowshoes all over that district looking for rich claims."

More typically, however, the spiritually advanced adventuress simply squandered her spoils on charitable causes—hospitals, church missions, and a continuously clamoring horde of down-on-your-luck colleagues. Indeed, friends claimed, she suffered from an addiction to doing good—an affliction far more expensive than a taste for fine whiskey or fancy women. Many, however, had reason to be grateful that she never tried to reform herself. "I never have had a word said to me out of the way," claimed the philanthropist in overalls; "The 'boys' would sure see to it that anyone whoever offered to insult me could never be able to repeat the offense."

By all reasonable standards, Cashman ought to have gotten to heaven sooner than she did. In Tombstone, she single-handedly rescued the owner of the Central Mining Company from a lynch mob. South of the border, she trekked solo across the desert sands in search of water, the only member of her ill-fated party strong enough to travel—and, it seems, the only one to receive (or so she claimed) the personal escort of "a good angel." Not everyone, however, was aware that Cashman was so well protected by celestial companions. In 1874, when she embarked upon a suicidal midwinter supply expedition to a remote camp in British Columbia, a squadron of soldiers was dispatched to retrieve her. They returned empty-handed, however, having found their prospective rescue bivouacked on an ice floe, "cooking her evening meal by the heat of a wood fire and humming a lively air."

Unlike their more rarefied cousins, however, earth angels don't live forever. "You never quite know," observed Cashman (who was spotted mushing a team of huskies across the snowfields of Alaska while in her sixties), "what's going to happen next, or when your time will come to cash in your checks." As to *where* she would be reaping her reward, however, the saintly gold-digger obviously had no doubt.

"When a woman behaves like a man, why doesn't she behave like a *nice* man?"
—Edith Evans

RADICAL RESCUERS AND MILITANT FEMINISTS

Ida Lewis (1842–1913)
Not Fishing for Compliments

Harper's magazine didn't know quite what to make of Ida Zoradia Lewis, a twenty-seven-year-old lighthouse keeper with a penchant for plucking drowning sailors from the turbulent ocean waters off Newport, Rhode Island. "Are we to believe that it is "feminine" for young women to row boats in storms?" inquired the perplexed publication in 1869; "Is it 'womanly' to tug and strain through a tempest, and then pull half-drowned men into a skiff?"

The heroine of Lime Rock Lighthouse had embarked on her death-defying career some ten years previously, when she scooped four young boys (nonswimmers all) out of the sea. In 1866, she retrieved the proverbial drunken sailor; in 1867, it was three Irish sheepherders (plus one prize-winning sheep) whom she rescued from a watery grave. And two years later, she rowed half a mile during a severe winter squall to snatch two submerged soldiers from the chill clutches of Poseidon—a feat that would eventually garner her a Congressional Medal of Honor.

As those who owed their lives to Ms. Lewis (ultimately some twenty-two in number, not counting barnyard animals) were no doubt gratified to note, *Harper's* finally determined that a temporary lapse from ladylike passivity was permissible in cases of extreme emergency. More important, it seems, it also determined that the angel of the Atlantic was slender, blue-eyed, and apparently unattached. Soon a deluge of intriguing proposals from potentially hydrophobic gentlemen came flooding through the mails, and in 1870, Lewis pledged her troth to a Connecticut fisherman. The marriage foundered, however, when Lewis concluded that she preferred the company of her six cats and cocker spaniel to that of her husband, and she never again ventured onto the stormy sea of love.

Nonetheless, rafts of rubberneckers (one of whom had to be rescued when her boat overturned en route) kept rowing their way to Lime Rock Lighthouse to gawk at America's most attractive daredevil. "Just now, Ida Lewis is the fashion," gushed Elizabeth Cady Stanton, who bragged that she had discussed the future of feminism with the lady of the lighthouse; "No one thinks of visiting Newport without seeing her."

By this point, however, Lewis was thoroughly tired of the steady stream of visitors and wanted nothing more than to be left alone. "They bother dreadfully when I have washing or cooking to do," she complained, unable to fully fathom her appeal to a heroine-hungry nation. "If there were some people out there who needed my help, I would go to them even if I knew I couldn't get back. Wouldn't you?"

> "We have only one life to live, and when our time comes, we've got to go; so it doesn't matter how."
>
> —I. L.

Harriet Tubman (circa 1820–1913)
Personal Trainer

Harriet Tubman, conductor-in-chief of the Underground Railroad, expected her passengers to be ready to ride when she pulled into the station. "You'll be free or die," she informed fearful fugitives, prodding them with her pistol to emphasize the point. Nothing in Tubman's own background, after all, had prepared her to empathize with the faint of heart. At thirteen, she intervened to protect another slave from an overseer; scars on her skull would always attest to that battle. In her twenties, she wrote her own passport from bondage, fleeing from Maryland to Philadelphia alone and unaided. The following year, she risked her life to rescue her sister, and a few months later, her brother. Complimented by John Brown as "the most of a man, naturally, that I ever met with," "General Tubman" absolutely refused to cater to the cowardly.

While others argued the pros and cons of revolution, the ad hoc abolitionist simply acted; stealing slaves, she believed, was the most logical strategy for smashing the South's "peculiar institution." Hiding in the woods or fields outside a plantation, she notified prospective passengers of her presence by humming a hymn or sending a coded message: "Tell my brothers to be always watching unto prayer," read one such cryptic communique; "When the good old ship of Zion comes along, be ready to step on board."

Few plantation owners, however, cottoned to the prospect of their "property," worth up to a thousand dollars a head, sailing away at will. In Maryland, where Tubman conducted an estimated nineteen rescues missions, peeved chattel holders convened regularly to discuss the personnel problem; at the height of her notoriety, there was a $40,000 price on her head. But of the scores she spirited away during the decade preceding the Civil War—no less than sixty slaves, and possibly as many as three hundred—it was her boast that she never once "lost a passenger."

As a teenager, Tubman had once dreamed of the Mason-Dixon line and the fertile fields blooming to the north. "Beautiful white ladies stretched out their arms to me over the line," she recalled. But their efforts were of no use, and anyway, it was only a dream. In real life, the first lady of liberation knew, she could rely only on herself—and, perhaps, the persuasive powers of her pistol—to engineer an escape to freedom.

A TRUE ESCAPE ARTIST

"There was one of two things I had a right to, liberty
or death; if I could not have one, I would have
the other; for no man should take me alive."

—H. T.

Sarah Winnemucca (1844–1891)
Return of the Native

Like every petite Piute in the mid-1800s, Indian rights activist Sarah Winnemucca was taught to fear the white man. "Our mothers told us that the whites were killing everybody and eating them," she recalled in *Life Among the Paiutes*, published in 1883. On the basis of this belief, the tribe deemed it prudent to bury its children beneath the ground whenever Caucasians were in the area: "Our mothers...planted sage bushes over our faces to keep the sun from burning them, and there we were left all day."

But Winnemucca's grandfather, chief of the nomadic Nevada tribe, pooh-poohed the putative dangers posed by palefaces; to him, they were "long-lost brothers," with their coming prophesied by ancient legend. At his insistence, young Winnemucca was sent to board with a white businessman and his family, who tutored her in English and evidently did not express any undue interest in cannibalism. Thus reassured, she went on to serve as an Indian language interpreter for the US government, and she was even occasionally spotted kicking up her heels at a predominantly white Washoe County saloon. "As there were but three white women in the town," one local racist later rationalized, "it was necessary...to take in Miss Sarah Winnemucca, the Piute Princess." Despite this accommodation, he added, "all danced with ardor and filled the air with splinters from the puncheon floor."

But thanks to the Bannock Uprising of 1878, in which hundreds of her people were taken captive by the adversarial tribe for which the rebellion was named, Winnemucca would not go down in history as just another Piute party girl. As a volunteer scout for the US Army, she tracked the fleeing Bannocks over a hundred miles of rough desert terrain, infiltrated the enemy camp, and under cover of dinnertime chaos, liberated over half the hostages—her own father among them. "That was the hardest work I ever did for the government in all my life," sighed the saddle-sore scout, whose efforts earned her five hundred dollars and an official invitation to lead further sorties for Uncle Sam.

But though the incident made Winnemucca the country's most popular Native American since Pocahontas, it did little to improve the lot of the Piutes. Apparently incapable of distinguishing between the Bannocks and their blameless captives, the Army rounded up those recently rescued and packed them off to a Washington prison camp. Only after Winnemucca paid a personal call on the secretary of the interior in 1880 were the government's disgruntled guests finally released. Weary of embodying the sole official exception to the rule that the only virtuous Indian was the deceased variety, the unhappy heroine withdrew to a Nevada reservation in 1883. There she passed her remaining years as a schoolteacher, no doubt providing her students with a somewhat different interpretation of Native American history than the whitewashed version that passed for the truth in other US classrooms.

"I, only an Indian woman, went and saved my father and his people."

—S. W.

Eve's Idea of Eden

In 1866, Martha McWhirter of tiny Belton, Texas, got the nod from God to found a quasi-religious commune for females only. Much to the dismay of many a Belton burgher, a stint as a so-called "Sanctificationist" soon became the rage among trendy local ladies. The stylish separatists who flocked to McWhirter's rural retreat plowed fields by day, pored over great literature by night, and never, ever, gave a second thought to perpetuating the species. Indeed, at least fifty fed-up feminists so enjoyed the self-sufficient solely-sisters society that they never again shouldered the cumbersome cross of the heterosexual housewife.

Sarah Emma Edmonds (1841–1898)
The Best Man for the Job

Even back in the Civil War era, a good man was hard to find; or at least so claimed Sarah Emma Edmonds, a chronic cross-dresser from Canada with a rather low opinion of the more hirsute gender. "When I look around and see the streets crowded with strong, healthy young men who ought to be foremost in the ranks of their country's defenders, I am not only ashamed, but I am indignant!" she wrote.

And perhaps just a trifle jealous. As Edmonds admitted in her bestselling autobiography, *Nurse and Spy in the Union Army*, it rankled in her soul that "male effeminates who never smelt powder on a battlefield" should so casually squander their gender-given right to swashbuckler. "What part am I to act in this great drama?" she demanded—and promptly enlisted in the Union Army under the name of Frank Thompson.

For the next two years, "the beardless boy" (as Edmonds was known to her gullible good buddies in the Michigan regiment) proceeded to give new meaning to the slogan "Be all that you can be." Frequently assigned to serve as a spy, the entirely bogus male infiltrated the Confederate camp in the guise of a boyish Black cook. (Happily, the outcome of that mission was more successful than her biscuits.) For another sortie into enemy territory, the woman warrior double-disguised herself quite convincingly as a rheumy-eyed old crone. Then there was her self-appointed role as a kind of kamikaze nurse-cheerleader at the bedsides of the mortally wounded. ("A glorious victory!" she exulted as one martyr to the Union cause expired in her "manly" arms.)

As she later revealed, soldier-boy Edmonds was no novice drag king; her pre-war resume included a stint as a door-to-door Bible salesman who "came near marrying a pretty little girl who was bound I should not leave Nova Scotia without her." Unfortunately for students of the gentlemanly arts, Edmonds failed to explain how she managed to disentangle herself from the clutches of her would-be inamorata. One presumes that it bore little resemblance to her technique for deflecting the attentions of a pistol-waving "rebel vixen," whom she calmly shot through the hand.

The chivalric code demanded no such kid-glove treatment of problematic males, however. Thus Edmonds felt perfectly free to empty her revolver in the face of a handsome captain of the Confederacy, eliminating (as she rather gleefully recalled) "a part of his nose and nearly half of his upper lip." Still, it seems that beneath her blood-spattered uniform beat a telltale tender heart: Edmonds later confessed, "I was sorry, for the graceful curve of his mustache was sadly spoiled."

"We're looking for a few good men."

—Campaign slogan for the US Marines

"I am naturally fond of adventure, a little ambitious, and a good deal romantic."

—S. E.

Anna Carroll (1815–1893)
The Spurned Strategist

Females, as the saga of Maryland military strategist Anna Carroll illustrates, aren't the only fickle gender. In July of 1861, forty-six-year-old Carroll found herself the unlikely darling of Abraham Lincoln's cabinet. Previously a speech writer for the short-lived Know-Nothing party and an enthusiastic correspondent with the press, she wowed the White House with her saucy unsolicited *Reply* to secessionist senators. By way of thanks, she received $1,250 in cash and the ardent admiration of Thomas A. Scott, the assistant secretary of war. And Lincoln himself was so enamored of her subsequent submission, "The War Powers of the General Government," that he placed it at the top of every congressman's required reading list. (That endorsement was by no means illogical; according to one Civil War scholar, Carroll's work contained "the best and most persuasive contemporary rationalizations of the theory upon which Lincoln acted.")

Four months after penning the popular *Reply*, the prolific pamphleteer presented Assistant War Secretary Scott with yet another unsolicited manuscript, this one setting forth the results of her research on the matter of military strategy. Contrary to the prevailing theory that control of the Mississippi was crucial to a Union victory, she concluded that the Tennessee River, which ran through the heart of the South, was more vital. And indeed, by February 1863, Ulysses S. Grant was marching down the Tennessee Valley, just as Carroll had suggested, clearing the way for Sherman's ultimate victorious stroll to the sea.

Under the circumstances, the Congress-charmer believed she was entitled to compensation for her proposal and lost no time in petitioning the President for $50,000. In this particular matter, however, her thoughts were distinctly out of joint with his: as far as the government was concerned, Grant had officially proposed the plan; therefore, obviously, he had also devised it. Terming Carroll's demand "the most outrageous one ever made to any government upon earth," Lincoln granted her $750 as a nuisance fee and sent her packing. And eight years later, Congress was equally disinclined to award the $250,000 which she claimed at that point for authoring the Tennessee campaign.

Carroll was to devote the subsequent fourteen years of her life to petitioning the government for recognition—to absolutely no avail. Nor did the endorsement of suffragists (themselves not a particularly persuasive portion of the population) who championed her cause in the 1880s lend an air of authenticity to her claim. To this day, historians continue to clash over the issue of Carroll's role in the Civil War, but even her detractors must concede that she never received her due. If the Tennessee proposal was hers and hers alone, she deserved recognition for formulating one of the most important military strategies of the Civil War. And if it wasn't, she deserved a Purple Heart for sheer unmitigated gall.

"A great humanitarian and a close friend of Abraham Lincoln."
—*Inscription on A. C.'s tombstone*

Eye for Eye, Tooth for Tooth

Even in the 1880s, public transportation seemed to bring out the worst in men. Weary of the leers of railway Romeos, one Miss Sperry of San Francisco vowed to take revenge. Finding herself seated opposite yet another ogler, the exasperated passenger withdrew behind a newspaper, extracted a glass eyeball and a set of pointy false teeth from her purse, and made a few covert adjustments. Needless to say, the startling transformation from vamp to vampire cleared Sperry's compartment of lecherous onlookers in a hurry.

Pauline Cushman (1833–1893)
The Perils of a POW

Like the heroine of a romance novel, actress Pauline Cushman possessed a penchant for improbably dramatic diversions. Depending on the year (and sometimes her mood), the dark-eyed, dishy stage star was also a spy, a self-defense expert, and finally, just another soldier wounded in the battle of love.

None of Cushman's widely publicized (albeit often by herself) escapades, however, seized the public imagination more fiercely than her stint as an uncommonly pulchritudinous prisoner of war. Audiences packed theaters nationwide in the mid-1860s to view the glamour girl's own dramatic reenactment of her capture by Confederate soldiers. Unable to explain the presence of certain incriminating battle plans in her boot, she had been court-martialed and sentenced to die. "Am I to be short, like a soldier, or die the death of a malefactor?" she inquired in the drama's cliff-hanging denouement. Fortunately, if predictably, she would succumb to neither grim fate: Just in the nick of time, Union forces stepped in and saved her lovely neck.

Soon "The Little Major" (or so an admiring Abraham Lincoln dubbed her) was much in demand to play military roles on stage, and reporters dogged her every move. Cushman had, it was noted, dumped a bowl of boiling soup on a boor "too hypnotized by her swarthy beauty" to mind his manners. She had also, according to the *San Francisco Chronicle*, horsewhipped an oaf who insulted her virtue. ("She kept him there meanwhile by holding a cocked pistol in her left hand," the *Chronicle* added helpfully, apparently eager to assist any reader wishing to attempt a similar feat.) Cushman-watchers were also touched to learn that as she came upon a teamster whipping his animals mercilessly, she drew her Winchester straight and true, commanding, "Unhitch those mules!"

But though fans might (and did) fawn *ad nauseam*, the rather indifferent spouse whom Cushman acquired in 1879 was not so mesmerized by her charms. In a last-ditch effort to inspire some passion in her partner, she left town for a spell, returning triumphantly with a baby in her arms. Unfortunately, the infant did not survive, and the marriage likewise foundered when the baby's biological mother (from whom, it turned out, Cushman had purchased the child) showed up to collect the corpse. Unlike any romance novel ever written, Cushman's dramatic story ended not in love and glory, but alone in a squalid San Francisco hotel. The coroner's certificate read: "Death from morphine taken not with suicidal intent, but to relieve pain." On a brighter note, observed one obituarist, her life had been "somewhat irregular for some years."

"Tell me the worst!"

—P. C.

FEARLESS FRONTIERSWOMEN

Tabitha Brown (1780–1858)

Pennies from Heaven

At the age of sixty-six, schoolteacher Tabitha Brown wasn't ready for the rest home yet. "God had a work for me to do," she wrote, "and had seen fit to use me to accomplish His own purposes." Possibly Ms. Brown—a Missouri widow weighing barely a hundred pounds—misunderstood the nature of this divine request. Or possibly the Lord was just doing his moving-in-mysterious-ways thing again. In any event, according to Brown, she received specific orders in 1846 to travel to "Paradise" (as son Orus termed Oregon's winsome Willamette Valley) via wagon train.

The pilgrim's progress, however, was not without rough patches. Just six hundred miles out of Oregon City, Brown recalled, her party was "decoyed off by a rascally fellow, assuring us that he had found a near cut-off." Instead, he swiftly stripped them of their possessions and left the impoverished pioneers wandering in the wilderness. "Our sufferings from that time no tongue can tell," declared Brown, who tried anyway. "We had sixty miles of desert without grass or water, mountains to climb, cattle giving out, wagons breaking, emigrants sick and dying, hostile Indians to guard against."

Four harrowing months later, the bedraggled band finally reached the safe harbor of Salem, Oregon. But the promised land wasn't exactly overflowing with milk and honey—there were, Brown noted, few compelling career opportunities for a chronologically advanced female in "a young man's country." (As usual, God had been rather vague on the subject of finances.) With her last coin, which she discovered stashed in an old glove, she invested in three needles, "traded off some of my old clothes to the squaws for buckskin, and worked it into gloves for the Oregon ladies and gentlemen." For her efforts, Brown netted thirty dollars.

But though that small sum saved her from starvation, the devout dowager couldn't help concluding that her Maker was unfortunately quite the consummate miser. "Why has Providence frowned at me and left me poor in this world?" she complained. "Had He blessed me with riches... I should establish myself in a comfortable house and receive all poor children and be a mother to them." Whether or not the heavens heeded that pocketbook prayer remains a matter of conjecture. In any event, Brown's words were not wasted on human ears: A missionary friend promptly provided her with funds to launch the first boarding school in the Oregon territory. Almost immediately, that enterprise attracted forty students, and in 1854, at the age of seventy-four, the much-praised principal received a charter to found the academy known today as Pacific University.

Counting her blessings toward the end of her life (which included not only the twin institutions over which she presided but several cows that she "let out for their milk and one-half the increase"), Brown attributed her worldly success to "my own industry and good management." Oddly enough, she completely forgot to thank the Lord.

"I have labored hard for myself and the public and the rising generation. I now have quit hard work and live at my ease."

—T. B.

Fanny Kelly (1845–?)
Brave Survivor

Captured in 1864 by a band of 250 Sioux warriors, Fanny Kelly didn't waste time worrying about the proverbial "fate worse than death." To the nineteen-year-old newlywed, who had just recently embarked upon the adventure of adulthood in the wilds of Wyoming, anything was better than staring the Grim Reaper square in the eye. "It is only those who have looked over the dark abyss of death," Kelly would later write, "who know how the soul shrinks from meeting the unknown future."

Nonetheless, the pragmatic pioneer's first act as a captive could scarcely be recommended as superlative survival strategy. Unlike an understandably fretful friend, she knew better than to draw attention to herself by raising a ruckus. But when noise-conscious Chief Ottowa threatened to silence the weeping woman, Kelly found it impossible to hold her tongue. "Perhaps it was a selfish thought of future loneliness in captivity which induced me to intercede," she later admitted. Solitude, however, was scarcely to be Kelly's lot among the Sioux: Her chutzpah so impressed the head honcho that he promptly laid down his knife and appointed himself the constant companion of his protesting prisoner (much to the annoyance, incidentally, of six preexisting wives).

Despite that auspicious beginning, however, the course of the cross-cultural relationship between chief and captive seldom ran smooth. One bone of contention was Ottowa's yen to transform his Caucasian companion into a tattooed Sioux sensation. But the frustrated exterior decorator was forced to postpone the experiment indefinitely—Kelly possessed, it turned out, a perplexing penchant for swooning whenever he hauled out the puncturing paraphernalia. She also caused him no end of trouble with his sextet of spouses, who tended to turn a tad homicidal when he referred to the interloper as the tribe's only "Real Woman." And try as he might, Ottowa simply couldn't forgive his stolen sweetheart for discarding a particularly precious peace pipe, a faux pas for which he deemed death the sole appropriate remedy. Only a cash bribe (Kelly having had the foresight to be carrying $120 in her purse at the time of her capture) served to assuage his wrath and save her skin.

Even after Ottowa surrendered his problematic pal to the US government, however, Kelly's trials didn't cease; an anxious nation could hardly wait for a woman "ravaged" by savages to spill the sordid details of her five-month ordeal. Those who hoped to hear tales of titillating tepee seductions were no doubt disappointed by her declaration that she had never "suffered from any of [the Sioux] the slightest personal or unchaste insult." Nevertheless, Ottowa's opportunistic ex-prisoner didn't shrink from embellishing her bestselling *Narrative of My Captivity Among the Sioux Indians* with a few highly picturesque particulars, subsequently surviving quite comfortably on the proceeds.

"While hope offers the faintest token of refuge, we pause upon the fearful brink of eternity and look back for rescue."

—F. K.

Nancy Kelsey (1823–1896)
An Unsettling Story

The pleasures of domesticity à deux entirely eluded poor Nancy Kelsey. For better or worse, the Missouri-born Mrs. never got the chance to stand by her man. Thanks to the whims of her ever-restless spouse, however, Ms. Kelsey did have the opportunity to trudge across scorching prairies, scale snowcapped mountain peaks, and fight off hostile Indians at his side.

It all started in 1841 when Mr. Kelsey, suffering from a severe case of wanderlust, signed on with the first party of pioneers to traverse the vast uncharted territory between St. Louis and California. To the astonishment of all, his eighteen-year-old bride—only recently recovered from the rigors of childbirth—promptly followed suit. "I could better endure the hardships of the journey than the anxieties for an absent husband," rationalized the teenage tenderfoot, the only woman among the group of thirty-three.

Demonstrating not only wifely devotion but also excellent equilibrium, Kelsey proceeded to cross the Sierra on foot with her infant daughter in her arms. "She bore the fatigues of the journey with...much heroism, patience, and kindness," one member of the party reported in his diary. But the saintly spouse scarcely had time to shake the dust off her boots before the travel bug again bit her husband in 1843 and they headed for the greener pastures of Oregon. This time, the journey featured an Indian raid: "I counted twelve of them as they went down before our guns," Kelsey recalled.

The following year found the family—now augmented by the birth of another baby—en route to California's Napa Valley. Once again, they were to run afoul of irritable Native Americans: "While the arrows were flying into our camp," Kelsey reported, "I took one babe and rolled it into a blanket and hid it in the brush and took my other child and hid it also." Subsequent action-packed road trips included jaunts to Mexico and Texas, where predictably enough, "we were attacked by Comanche Indians." Kelsey's oldest daughter, in fact, later died of injuries suffered in one such raid.

Still, the high-risk lifestyle was not entirely devoid of happier highlights: "I have baked bread for General Fremont and talked to Kit Carson," the wandering wife would later boast. Nor were explorers the only interesting species encountered in the wilderness; on occasion, Kelsey reported, she had also had the opportunity to "run from bear."

Death finally parted Kelsey from her peripatetic partner in 1888, and she retreated—no doubt with some relief—to a remote cabin in the Santa Barbara mountains. Neighbors recalled that the retired adventuress could still be counted on to "help bring a baby into the world, bind splints on a broken leg, or minister to a fever-ridden child." Unless her aid was so solicited, however, the well-traveled widow seldom ventured far from home. She had, she explained, already "had enough incidents happen to me to make a book."

"Among all the forms of absurd courage, the courage of girls is outstanding. Otherwise there would be fewer marriages."

—Colette

The Little Woman

Though she stood only thirty-two inches tall, Lavinia Warren never suffered from a shortage of admirers. Two thousand guests attended her 1863 wedding to Tom Thumb, including spurned suitor George Washington Morris Nutt, who may or may not have been among the genuine well-wishers. Following Thumb's death, the minute media sensation went on to wed Mr. Primo Magri, an equally diminutive (but far less famous) dwarf. Fortunately for the sake of marital harmony, miniscule Magri was man enough not to mind being known primarily as Mrs. Tom Thumb's second husband.

Mary Fields (1832–1914)
Too Big to Boss

Having spent her youth as a slave in Tennessee, Mary Fields had experienced more than enough obedience training for a lifetime when she stormed into Cascade, Montana, in 1884. Now, she made it clear, she was ready to call her own shots—and heaven help the brute who tried to bully her. Not that fifty-two-year-old Fields—a brawny six-footer who tipped the scales at two hundred pounds—looked like an easy woman to push around. In fact, turned out in trousers and chomping on the obligatory cigar, she didn't much look like anyone's idea of a nineteenth-century woman at all. Equally thought-provoking, it seems, was the fact that she routinely carried both a revolver and a rifle.

To the fearless Fathers who headed the Catholic foundation in Cascade, however, the hefty heat-packer simply looked like one hell of an employee. So for eight years, Fields earned her daily bread by doing most of the heavy work around the mission—loading supply wagons, hauling freight, and on one memorable occasion, fending off a pack of wolves. True, she seldom showed up for work without a jug of whiskey in tow. ("She could drink more than anyone I ever knew," one besotted admirer would later recall.) Nonetheless, there were few complaints about the way Fields discharged her duties. Discharging her rifle in the direction of a hired hand who insulted her, however, was another matter entirely. Turning the other cheek, suggested the mild-mannered monks, would have been a better solution, and they sent her packing.

In its infinite wisdom, however, the US government was happy to put an aging, trigger-happy Amazon on its payroll: As the driver of a US mail coach, Fields, now in her sixties, distinguished herself in any number of climatic conditions. But as she approached the age of seventy, even the West's toughest postwoman couldn't keep up the pace her profession demanded, and she grudgingly turned to the less taxing lifestyle of a laundress.

In the pre-Maytag era, however, that occupation still required a significant amount of stamina: Between washes, Fields—the only woman permitted by public ordinance to drink in the saloons of Cascade—maintained her muscle tone by hoisting a few with the boys. One day, she was exercising her personal privileges in a local dive when a customer who had neglected to pay his laundry bill happened by. Drawing herself up to her full height, the elderly washerwoman accosted the offending deadbeat, and with one swift blow, laid him flat on his back. Satisfying as that powerhouse punch must have been for Fields, no single triumph could ever compensate for the injustices of her early life. But at least one account—or so she announced to astonished onlookers—was now settled in full.

> "The thing women have to learn is that nobody gives you power. You just take it."
>
> —Roseanne Arnold

Martha Black (1866–1957)
A Woman's Nature

Some girls never do get the hang of the homemaker thing. When her family's Chicago château went up in flames in the great fire of 1871, five-year-old Martha Black didn't shed a tear. "I had always wanted to live outside," she explained in *My Seventy Years*, an autobiographical account of her meandering ascent to membership in the Canadian Parliament. But young Black was not to remain a happy camper. The horrid house was soon rebuilt, and she went on to endure all the standard rigors of young ladyhood: finishing school, debutante balls, and in 1887, the inevitable financially suitable mate.

Predictably, however, stodgy "Mr. Right" proved no proper soul mate for his wild-at-heart wife. In 1898, Black saw her chance to make her escape: Gold had been discovered in the Canadian Klondike, and thousands of restless citizens were swarming northward to seize a piece of the North American dream. "It looked like a great adventure, and I was consumed with the urge to have my part in it," she recalled. Her sissy spouse, however, appeared equally consumed with the urge to preserve his cozy urban lifestyle. "He went his way. I went mine. I never did see [him] again," she reported.

Perhaps Black would not have so boldly abandoned hearth and home had she realized at the time that she was pregnant. Oblivious to that fact, however, the newly single sourdough and her adventurous brother made their way to Skagway, there to embark upon the grueling journey over the Chilkoot Pass into the northwestern Yukon Territory. Known as "the worst trail this side of hell," that treacherous forty-two-mile footpath posed no small challenge to a man in his prime, let alone to an expectant mother. Still unaware of her "delicate condition," however, the 110-pound outdoorswoman attributed her discomfort during the hellacious hike solely to her stiff-boned corset and cumbersome long skirt. ("For God's sake...buck up and be a man!" Black's brother snapped when she collapsed, just once, in tears.) By the time she finally staked her coveted claim in the summer of 1898, the pregnant pioneer had also endured a spine-tingling river run through the "seething cauldron" of the White Horse Rapids, too many meals consisting chiefly of squirrel meat, and the alarming attentions of one boorish prospector who "casually offered to share his bunk with me." "But I had no fear of anything," gloated Black, "especially if I had a large stick." According to her, in fact, even single motherhood turned out to be a snap: "I was alone, [but] it was...an incredibly easy birth— Mother Nature's gift to women who live a natural out-of-door life such as I had done."

Over the course of the next several decades, Black would blaze a wide swath through the Yukon wilderness as a serial grubstaker, sawmill owner, avalanche dodger, and—when the necessity arose—bear killer. But not until seventy, at which age she triumphed over a male rival for a seat in the Canadian Parliament, would the happily displaced homemaker finally find a House large enough to accommodate her ambitions. "What I wanted," she explained, "was not shelter and safety, but liberty and opportunity.

THE CANADIAN PARLIAMENT BUILDING:
BETTER THAN A BURNED-DOWN HOUSE

"I knew that my path lay ahead, that there was no turning back now."

—M. B.

AUDACIOUS ARTISTS AND AD HOC ARCHITECTS

Lola Montez (1818–1861)
Kiss of the Spider Woman

All raven-tressed dancer Lola Montez wanted from King Ludwig I of Bavaria was permission to perform at a prestigious Munich theater. At least, that was the touring artiste's excuse for crashing the castle gates one day in 1847. But when the sixty-something got an eyeful of the exotic entertainer's celebrated cleavage, his attention wandered from the topic at hand. Was or was not, he demanded imperiously, that bountiful bosom entirely her own?

Lascivious Lola, whose name (not to mention body) had already been linked with a scandalous quantity of significant others—among them, Franz Liszt and the czar of Russia—saw no need to reply. Instead, she seized a pair of scissors, and with one swift slash, revealed all. Soon the pseudo-Spanish seductress (née Maria Dolores Eliza Rosanna Gilbert of Limerick, Ireland) was the primary paramour of the monarch, and a bona fide baroness to boot.

Perhaps Ludwig—twice Lola's age—wasn't the most boisterous of bedmates. Still, he was quick to cover a check, especially the kind Montez liked to sign as "The King's Mistress." In 1848, however, when his concubine suddenly sprouted a social conscience and started chattering about radical reform, Ludwig concluded she had grown too big for her bustier and bounced her right out of Bavaria.

Unable to secure another position as a kept woman, Montez polished up her professional moves and transported them back to liberty-loving

America. But New York City audiences merely squirmed in their seats when she showed off her brand-new "Spider Dance," a sensuous, writhing impression of a maiden tangled in an invisible web. Even the most avant-garde Easterners had to admit that the climax of the piece—a fit of agonized arachnid convulsions—rather exceeded the bounds of good taste.

But San Francisco, where the chesty chorine debuted *à la arantella* in 1853, didn't give a fig leaf for dreary convention. "Higher! Higher!" roared the culture mavens of that mostly male metropolis as Montez groped beneath her skirts for some suggestively straying spider. True, European royalty had more class, and arguably, more money. But no one ever embraced the frenzied femme (who by now was puffing on cigars and kept a bear cub as a pet) so enthusiastically as the carnal kings of the California gold bonanza. Recognizing a kindred spirit, they clasped her to their collective chest and held her there like a long-lost daughter. (Well, perhaps not quite like a *daughter*.)

"I was always notorious; never famous."

—L. M.

Harriet Hosmer (1830–1908)
Portrait of the Artist as a Young Woman

For the budding nineteenth-century artist, a set of breasts constituted a distinct professional liability. Those capable of perpetuating the species, it was felt, were honor bound to do so—a dictate which generally precluded the wholehearted pursuit of more idiosyncratic passions. But Harriet Hosmer, touted in her era as the most significant sculptor of her sex, could muster little enthusiasm for the purely procreative lifestyle. For the female who fancied herself a serious artist, she proclaimed, "Marriage is a moral wrong...for she must either neglect her profession or her family, becoming neither a good wife and mother nor a good artist." And, she added, "My ambition is to become the latter, so I wage eternal feud with the consolidating knot."

A rebel of the more robust variety, Hosmer spent her wonder years scaling mountains (including the Missouri peak which bears her name) and sailing solo down the Mississippi, once pausing along the way to pass a peace pipe with a group of Dakota Indians. By the time she set up shop in a Rome studio in 1852, the aerobically accomplished artist had seen more of life than most young ladies her age. Owing to a covert series of private anatomy lessons from a St. Louis physician, she had also seen a great many more bodies in the buff than most maidens. Needless to say, her professional passion for that genre soon sparked the outrage of a society which could scarcely bring itself to call a limb a leg and which buried the female figure under yards of flowing fabric. "Her want of modesty is enough to disgust a dog," carped one critic, evidently more concerned with Hosmer's morality than her merits as an artist. "She has casts for the entire *female model* made and exhibited in a shockingly indecent manner for all the young artists who called upon her."

To the more romantically inclined, however, there was nothing even slightly sordid about Hosmer's obsession with her putatively improper profession. "She lives here all alone (at ago twenty-two)," gushed the poet Elizabeth Barrett Browning, "dines and breakfasts at the cafes precisely as a young man would; works from six o'clock in the morning till night as a great artist must." A happily confirmed spinster to the end of her days, Hosmer went on to reap international acclaim for her monumental statues celebrating the forms of famous females from Queen Isabella to Zenobia. True, traditionalists would maintain well into the twentieth century that aesthetically inclined ladies should limit themselves to decorating teacups in the drawing room. Following Hosmer's lead, however, a bold new generation of artists both refused to squander their talents painting posies and did not allow bouts of childbearing to circumscribe their chosen careers. As the single-minded sculptor illustrated in her own graphic fashion, anatomy—contrary to popular opinion—need not actually be destiny.

THE BEAUTIFUL HARRIET

"Even if so inclined, an artist has no business to marry."
—H. H.

Home Ergonomics

Tired of living in the house that Jack built, North Carolina housewife Harriet Irwin decided to design the domicile of her dreams. In 1869, the happy homemaker received the first US architectural patent granted to a woman for her "hexagonal building" plan. The six-sided structure (a shape "of greater artistic beauty than the square," according to the self-taught architect) featured a continuous circle of interconnecting chambers to enhance "communication between the different rooms." Iconoclastic Irwin also designed her own hexagonal gravestone, possibly hoping to improve communication between the different tombs.

Loie Fuller (1862–1928)
Light on Her Feet

"People have the idea that I am such an occult, mystical, ethereal sort of creature," complained down-to-earth dancer Loie Fuller, who made her rather prosaic public debut as a child temperance lecturer in Illinois. And although Fuller's radiant stage presence would one day electrify turn-of-the-century Paris, she readily admitted that her brilliance derived from technological innovation in lighting effects rather than virtuosity of technique. "I am the personification of the practical," proclaimed the humble prima donna.

Nonetheless, one imaginative critic found that Fuller, draped in yards of diaphanous gauze "which rose and fell in phosphorescent waves," resembled nothing so much as "a huge glistening moth, wandering in obscurity." Marie Curie sighed that "Loie had a delicate soul," and refused only with the greatest regret Fuller's request for "butterfly wings of radium." (Despite her disappointment, Fuller was soon to create the world's first—and, one strongly suspects, final—"Radium Dance" in Curie's honor.) And the admiration of young Isadora Duncan, whose style would be significantly influenced by the older dancer, knew no bounds. "Before our very eyes she turned to many-colored shining orchids," gushed Duncan, "to a wavering sea-flower, and at length to a spiral-like lily, all magic of Merlin, the sorcery of light, color, flowing form."

Despite such hyperbolic hoopla, however, Fuller—who never appeared without a team of fourteen electricians, cued by subtle taps of her heel—owed far more to modern chemistry than to alchemy. Most particularly, she prided herself on developing a method for treating fabric with phosphorescent salts to give it a "strong and beautiful glow." "Part of my hair was blown off in an explosion while I was experimenting in my laboratory," she shrugged, "...but I do not care.

I suppose I am the only person known as a dancer but who has a personal preference for Science."

THE "GLISTENING MOTH" STALKING THE STAGE

"I do not save for my old age. I do not care what happens then."

—L. F.

When Good Women Go Bad

Devoted for decades to the proper pursuits of the Victorian homemaker, fifty-year-old Ellen Peck suddenly plunged from her pedestal one day in 1880. After bilking a millionaire of his bonds, the fledgling felon offered him her services as a private investigator, hauling in several hefty payments before her client caught on to the con. That was just for starters; during her subsequent thirty-odd years of life, the aging adventuress managed to carve out a supremely successful career in the burgeoning field of fraud. Nor did the occasional stint behind bars dampen Peck's enthusiasm for the larcenous lifestyle. Formerly a frustrated housewife, she evidently preferred doing time to doing dishes.

Frances Johnston (1864–1952)
Radical Review

"Beauty is truth, truth beauty," wrote Keats in 1817. But by the mid-Victorian era, etiquette-conscious citizens on either side of the Atlantic could scarcely look each other in the eye. "A lady, declared *Our Deportment* in 1882, "will always fail to hear that which she should not hear." Verbal vagueness was much in vogue; an elaborate symbology of flowers mumbled the words that timid tongues dared not utter. And the frankly female figure, once a subject worthy of the Western world's greatest artists, disappeared altogether beneath hip-hiding hoops, a plethora of petticoats and ruffles contributing to the deliberate confusion.

Against the backdrop of that neo-puritanical mania for prettification, the uncompromising vision of Frances Johnston, the nation's first famous female photographer, appears all the more remarkable. Trained as a painter in Paris, twenty-three-year-old Johnston purchased one of the first Kodak cameras from George Eastman in 1887 and was soon putting it to good use in the service of photojournalism. Photography, she claimed, was "the more accurate medium," and her camera did not lie: Through bold black-and-white imagery, the socially progressive photographer argued the case of the impoverished Pennsylvania coal miner, the oppressed female factory worker, and the controversial cause of higher education for Black Americans.

But there was more to Johnston than a one-dimensional visual polemicist. Noted for her portraits of Mark Twain and Susan B. Anthony, she wandered through the White House every few years, snapping several generations of first ladies (and a few of their gentlemen as well). She offered both technical and emotional support to budding lady shutterbugs and organized an exhibition of American women photographers for the Paris Exposition in 1900.

And as the brightest light in DC's bohemian social scene, she eagerly experimented with artsy innovations—and evidently not in the photographic realm alone. As apprentice Mattie Hewitt intimated in her letters, Johnston was not always—unlike the "nice little man" Hewitt had married—too busy for amorous "nonsense."

The celebrated camerawoman, however, never suggested any such thing. A painfully polite correspondent, she did not distinguish herself in her prose, which bore the imprint of the era into which she was born.

But in her chosen medium, Johnston did not shrink from mocking the warped Victorian view of womanhood. A smoldering cigarette, a brazen beer stein, a shocking stretch of exposed limb—all these, flaunted in her deliberately unconventional self-portrait of 1896, spoke volumes about the choices a woman might make, if only she dared. But most of all, it was the angular, unabashedly assertive lines of Johnston's body as she leaned forward to face the future that revealed a very un-Victorian truth: A picture need not be pretty to be powerful, nor a woman passive to be beautiful.

"Learn early the immense difference between the photograph that is merely a photograph and that which is also a picture."

—F. J.

Lillian Russell (1861–1922)
Much Admired

To writer Edna Ferber, the famous full-blown figure of diva Lillian Russell resembled a roller coaster. To a more poetically minded critic from the *New York World*, her undulating curves were "so many sonnets of motion." But to most Americans in the latter two decades of the nineteenth century, rotund Russell—the most photographed woman of her generation—simply represented the epitome of feminine beauty.

Ill-suited to the role of shrinking Victorian violet, Russell reveled in a lifestyle as flamboyant as the lush lines of her body suggested. In an era when a rare glimpse of a feminine ankle sent male minds reeling, she mounted the stage in scandalously short skirts, her sturdy legs showcased in purple tights. Indifferent to the stares of strangers, she rolled through Central Park on a gold-plated bicycle, its spokes studded with diamonds, rubies, and emeralds. And in 1890, her well-known voice was the first to waft over the new long-distance wires, warbling an operatic air into the far-off ear of President Benjamin Harrison.

Naturally, a nation that worshipped at the altar of Russell's avoirdupois hungered to know her beauty secrets. Obligingly, the press reported that the gorgeous gourmand (an Iowa girl born and bred) liked nothing better for lunch than a platter of corn on the cob followed by crêpes suzette. Her solution to the dessert dilemma was duly noted: She chose both cantaloupe *and* ice cream. And it was a proud day for fans of feminine flesh when she challenged outrageously outsized Diamond Jim Brady to a conspicuous consumption contest in which she matched him bite for bite.

Nor did the dining room constitute the sole forum for the indulgence of Russell's rather Amazonian appetites. One husband would not suffice, nor even two; by her third foray into matrimony, however, even the sensual singer was sated, skipping the customary postnuptial pleasures in favor of a brisk poker game. ("I *always* play cards on my wedding night," she yawned.) But not only her bridegroom lay awake in the dark, longing for Lillian to come to bed. Tormented by unrequited love for the voluptuous vocalist (whom he had never met in person), a New York machinist plunged to his death at Niagara Falls.

And a Nevada man shot and killed the infidel who refused to admit that Russell was the most beautiful woman in the world; this, the jury ruled, constituted justifiable homicide.

By today's post-Twiggy standards, it seems peculiar that the person who inspired such desperate passions, though only five feet, six inches tall, tipped the scales at a zaftig 165 pounds. But in the extravagant gilded age, the ectomorphic individual was considered merely peculiar, or possibly impoverished—certainly not morally superior. "There was nothing wraithlike about Lillian Russell," recalled one wistful admirer, long after tastes had turned toward a more compact format. "We liked that."

> "You ought to try to eat raw oysters in a restaurant
> with every eye focused on you. It makes you feel
> as if the creatures were whales, your fork a derrick,
> and your mouth the Mammoth Cave."
>
> —L. R.

Sarah Winchester (1839–1922)
Haunted Homemaker

Though architect-by-accident Sarah Winchester was on intimate terms with the drawing room, she spent a full four decades without making the acquaintance of a drafting board. But when husband George, scion of the repeating-rifle Winchester family, died in 1880, a Boston psychic informed the twenty-million-dollar widow that she had also inherited her spouse's staggering spiritual debt to the dead. Consequently, the soothsayer revealed, it was now her obligation to construct an opulent pleasure palace as a rendezvous point for souls who had succumbed to a fatal bullet. As an added incentive, the psychic promised, Winchester herself would elude death so long as that convention center of the occult remained under construction.

As to the consequences of noncompliance, the unhappy heiress, who swallowed this peculiar prophecy lock, stock, and barrel, evidently drew her own conclusions. In 1882, she fled to San Jose, California, and unencumbered by any architectural training whatsoever (though she evidently *could* read in Turkish) embarked upon her Sisyphean spiritual task. Construction of the eternally expanding manse she called the Llanada Villa would occupy the next forty years of her life, five million dollars of her fortune, and the rapt attention of her astonished neighbors. Sparing no expense in her campaign to appease the deceased, Winchester outfitted that sprawling 160-room maze with Tiffany cut-glass doors, crystal chandeliers, and a trio of elevators for wraiths who preferred an entirely effortless form of transport. Other blandishments to blithe spirits included secret passageways, trap doors, staircases leading nowhere, and myriad other occult—or perhaps merely inept—oddities. (According to some, Winchester simply failed to correct one architectural blunder before moving on to the next.)

In any event, the hospitality of Llanada Villa was enjoyed exclusively, if at all, by invisible visitors: Mere mortals received a chilly welcome indeed from the reclusive heiress. President Theodore Roosevelt was rudely rebuffed when he came to call in 1903; many a less lofty guest was exorcised by a pack of bloodhounds roaming restlessly about the grounds. Even agile Harry Houdini couldn't quite manage to slip past security.

Little evidence exists, however, to indicate that Llanada ever really became quite the hotbed of hobgoblins it was intended to be. True, neighbors once reported some ghastly sounds emanating from the house. Upon investigation, however, it turned out that Winchester herself was the auditory offender, exercising her arthritic fingers with a handsaw. Furthermore, the Boston psychic proved dead wrong on one crucial point: Though Winchester kept her end of the bargain faithfully, never ceasing construction for a day, she nonetheless passed over to the other side at the age of eighty-three. Like the vast majority of departed souls, the bizarre blueprinter proved a remarkably poor communicator, and nothing is known of her reception in the hereafter. She was, however, remembered fondly by a few well-paid construction workers who devoted their entire careers to executing her demonic designs and retired quite handsomely off the proceeds of her worldly wealth.

"Prophecy is the most gratuitous form of error."

—George Eliot [née Mary Ann Evans]

SHOCKING SCHOLARS AND WANTON WORDSMITHS

Delia Bacon (1811–1859)
How to Broadside a Bard

"Men," as Shakespeare may possibly have written, "should be what they seem." Scholar Delia Bacon, who had been sadly disappointed in love, embraced that sentiment wholeheartedly. The only problem was that the brainy New England bluestocking (who once beat out Edgar Allan Poe in a short story contest) didn't believe in Shakespeare any more than she believed in Santa Claus. A self-educated expert on Elizabethan England, she doubted that the celebrated butcher's son was capable of spelling his own name, let alone penning the greatest masterpieces known to the Western world.

Long before she denounced the great bard as a fraud, however, Bacon realized that men were, in fact, not always what they seemed. At the age of thirty-five, while touring as a history lecturer, she succumbed to the charms of young Alexander MacWhorter, a Yale divinity student twelve years her junior. Naïve as a schoolgirl, Bacon naturally assumed that her one-and-only's intentions were honorable. Somehow, though, amorous Alexander never quite got around to discussing marriage, even after Bacon popped the question herself—five times, as a matter of fact.

"God does not need my labor, he appoints me to suffer," she wailed, and retreated to the library to lick her wounds. Who knows what transpired there among the dusty tomes? But by the time Bacon emerged, she had forgotten all about MacWhorter and was raging like a madwoman against her newest nemesis: William Shakespeare. Based on certain clues concealed deep within the famous plays, Bacon proclaimed, it was clear that the man she dubbed the "Stratford Poacher" was merely a poseur. The real geniuses, she added, were a group of worldly aristocrats led by Sir Francis Bacon (to whom she herself was not related—except, perhaps, in terms of literary erudition).

"You know perfectly well that the great world does not care a sixpence who wrote Hamlet," Delia Bacon's brother chided. But the conspiracy theory fascinated East Coast literati, including Ralph Waldo Emerson, who spearheaded a fundraising campaign to send Bacon to England for further research. The result, published in 1857, was a rambling seven-hundred-page volume titled *The Philosophy of the Plays of Shakespeare Unfolded*. It was also unanimously ill-received; even Nathaniel Hawthorne, who wrote the foreword, couldn't bring himself to read it all the way through.

Today, Bacon's theory (though not her writing style) enjoys greater credence in academic circles, having been espoused from time to time by prominent male scholars. Regrettably, however, her own contemporaries were little inclined to award an "A" for effort. Most characterized the daring debunker as an oddball egghead who simply cracked under the strain of a broken romance. And indeed, Bacon may well have been as hopelessly deranged as Hamlet himself. What nineteenth-century female in her right mind, after all, would dare challenge the authority of *any* man—let alone suggest that the emperor of the English language wore no clothes?

"What's in a name?"

—*William Shakespeare*

Carey Thomas (1857–1935)
School for Scandal

Today, the most risqué romantic fantasy of teenager Carey Thomas would scarcely elevate an eyebrow, let alone a heartbeat. But by the straitlaced standards of the 1870s, the scenario was utterly scandalous. As Thomas (the precedent-setting president of Bryn Mawr from 1894 to 1922) would later recall, the script revolved around two studious sweethearts ensconced in a library with "great big easy chairs where we could sit lost in books for days together."

Oh yes, and one other thing: Both of these imagined intellectuals were women. Oddly enough, however, that wasn't the element that provoked apoplexy in Thomas' Mom and Pop. Indeed, the love that dare not speak its name settled right down for a cozy chat in the Thomas household. "If only it were possible for women to elect women as well as men for a life's love!" the budding lesbian sighed to her mother, circa 1880. To which that hetero-yet-hip parent replied, not batting an eye: "[Your] feeling is quite natural. [We] used to have the same romantic love for our friends."

But if passion, Sapphic or otherwise, was the province of the female, the library that figured so prominently in Thomas' fantasy decidedly was not. Not, one understands, that she had ever made any secret of her shameful intellectual proclivities. "I ain't going to get married, and I don't want to teach school," she had announced as a child (fortunately, the grammar of the future academician would improve a great deal over the years). She would, she said, prefer it if God should kill her if she couldn't learn Greek and go to college. And just in case her meaning wasn't clear, she added emphatically: "I can't imagine anything worse than living a regular young lady's life."

Apparently such hints fell on deaf ears, however, for the Thomas family found their brainy offspring's decision to attend college "as shocking a choice as a life of prostitution." By now, however, their daughter was a hopeless case. Fully committed to the course of reckless intellectual pursuit, she went on to indulge her depraved adolescent desires to her heart's content. In 1882, accompanied by "devoted companion" and colleague Mary Gwinn, she took her PhD summa cum laude from the University of Zurich. Appointed president of Bryn Mawr at the age of thirty-seven, she didn't even have the decency to keep her controversial conviction that "girls can learn, can reason, can compete with men in the grand fields of literature, science, and conjecture" to herself. Instead, Thomas subjected fragile feminine minds to examinations as rigorous as those at Harvard, refused to make academic accommodations for ladies who lacked "mental discipline," and actually supplied her scholars with maids, freeing them from the gender-given obligation to clean up after themselves. Most audaciously of all, the profligate president lived openly with Ms. Gwinn on the college campus, probably even visiting the library with her from time to time.

"One man's mind differs from another man's mind far more widely than all women's minds differ from all men's."

—C. T.

Sara Parton, a.k.a. "Fanny Fern" (1811–1872)

The Writer's Revenge

"No happy woman ever writes," wrote journalist Sara Parton, who had reason to know. And indeed, as many a depressed diarist can attest, an angst-ridden soul is prone to voice her woes via the pen. But in 1855, when Parton published the scandalously autobiographical *Ruth Hall*, her caveat came with a corollary. No woman who wrote—so convention decreed—would remain content for long.

Not so, of course, the male who succumbed to the muse. Parton's father published the *Youth's Companion* with no untoward consequence. Brother Nathaniel edited the *New York Mirror* with impunity, and was celebrated, not deplored, as a poet. But when penniless Parton—once widowed, once divorced, and without future financial prospects—suggested that her work would reflect well on the *Mirror*, her brother termed her ambition "vulgar." A career as a seamstress, he suggested, was more in keeping with her talents. ("I have tried the unobtrusive employment," the far-from-fictitious Ruth Hall would later retort; "the wages are six cents a day.")

Regrettably, the family's party line was a familiar one in that unenlightened day: Even the hallowed Nathaniel Hawthorne had been heard fuming that female writers were nothing but "a damned mob of scribbling women." Nonetheless, Parton (publishing under the very proper nom de plume of Fanny Fern) met with some success in small Boston magazines, and in 1853, the collected *Fern Leaves from Fanny's Port-Folio* stunned nasty Nathaniels everywhere by becoming an immediate bestseller. To the chagrin of her churlish brother, Parton subsequently attracted the attention of the *New York Ledger*, where she was installed as a weekly columnist in 1855.

But when Fanny bared her fangs in *Ruth Hall*, her reputation as a "lady" writer was nearly ruined. Like Parton, the heroine of that no-holds-barred roman à clef was a widowed writer. Like Parton, she suffered from the slurs of an egotistical sibling (discreetly disguised under the delightful appellation of "Apollo Hyacinth"). And like Parton, Ruth Hall would savor the satisfaction of the ultimate snicker.

To fickle American audiences, however, the always-appealing "angry young man" genre did not translate well into a feminine format. "Ruthless Hall," outraged critics suggested, might have been a more apt title. Not only had the irate matron betrayed "unfeminine bitter wrath and spite," but she had "demeaned herself as no right-minded woman should have done." And the unexpected commendation of Nathaniel Hawthorne, who praised the novel's lack of "female delicacy," served as a distinctly dubious endorsement.

Bad notices, however, are better than none at all: Even as the scandal crested and broke, Parton's star at the *Ledger* continued to rise. For the rest of her life she would remain in its employ, one of the country's first female columnists, and at an unprecedented weekly salary of a hundred dollars, one of the best paid writers in the nation. Needless to say, for a "scribbling" woman to excel at the very thing she was expressly prohibited from doing was sweet revenge indeed. And to those of a literary bent, it could only be described as the most poetic justice possible.

"And now our heroine had become a regular business woman."

—S. P., *Ruth Hall*

Maria Mitchell (1818–1889)
Pi in the Sky

In 1847, amateur astronomer Maria Mitchell scanned the night skies over Nantucket, spotted a comet, and promptly calculated its exact position. Unfortunately, the thirty-year-old librarian's discovery was not universally well-received: Well-equipped male astronomers around the world were chagrined that they had been eclipsed by a woman with a tiny two-inch telescope. The king of Denmark, however, didn't give a hoot about Mitchell's gender or the fact that owing to a pressing need for cash, she merely moonlighted as a stargazer. He had promised a gold medal to anyone who discovered an unknown comet, and the offer still stood.

With both a heavenly body and a royal commendation to her name, Mitchell's professional opportunities, hitherto nonexistent, suddenly skyrocketed. The American Academy of Arts and Sciences drafted her as its first female member in 1848, and the American Association for the Advancement of Science soon followed suit. By 1865, Matthew Vassar, president of the newly founded Female College in New York, was recruiting her to serve as the star of his science department. Modestly, Mitchell demurred, pleading that she had no advanced education herself. In the end, however, she was seduced by his talk of a twelve-inch telescope—an offer no scientifically sensitive woman could refuse.

Not every gentleman was so generous, however. Many professional peers viewed the now-acclaimed astronomer as an anomaly, a curiosity rather than a colleague. Perhaps for this reason, Mitchell's lectures often conveyed a frankly feminist message. "We are women studying together," she reminded her Vassar students. "We cannot accept anything as granted beyond the first mathematical formulae. Question everything else." Implicitly included in "everything else," of course, was male supremacy in scientific endeavors.

Ardent young astronomers hesitated, however, to commit themselves to an arena where few females had distinguished themselves. "When I get home, no one there will take any interest in astronomy...and there will be no one to help me on," worried one. "When I think of it, I get discouraged."

But to Professor Mitchell, a former full-time librarian, the shortage of women in the sciences was neither a cosmic mystery nor a reason to flee the field. "Theories do not come by chance," she wrote. "They are not born of the hurry and worry of daily toil; they are diligently sought... And until women have given their lives to investigation, it is idle to discuss their capacity for original work." Thanks to Mitchell's own educational endeavors, however, the subject of scientists in skirts would soon be less moot: twenty-five of her students were eventually to find their names listed in *Who's Who in America*, many of them for achievements in the laboratory or observatory. Just as freethinking females had always known—and men were beginning to suspect— woman's destiny of intellectual inferiority was not written in the stars.

"No woman would say, 'I am but a woman!'
But a woman! What more can you ask to be?"

—M. M.

Emily Dickinson (1830–1886)

A Victorian Veto

"They say that 'home is where the heart is,' " wrote the enormously eccentric Emily Dickinson; "I think it is where the *house* is, and the adjacent buildings." And indeed, the "half-cracked poetess" (as one contemporary critic insisted on calling her) died in the same Amherst manor in which she was born, seldom venturing far afield in the fifty-six intervening years. Within that circumscribed realm, however, the radical recluse reigned supreme. Master of the English language and mistress of her own destiny, she would neither go out to court the mediocre masses nor admit them to her domain.

So jealously did Dickinson guard her privacy that only seven of her 1,775 poems were published in her lifetime—and those against her will. (Her preferred means of distribution was to sew her scribblings together in odd little bundles and secrete them away in trunks and drawers.) "How dreary to be someone," she shuddered. "How public like a frog / To sing your song the livelong day / To an admiring bog." She would not have her photograph taken. She would not address letters in her own hand. And the privileged few permitted to discourse with her were frequently ordered to communicate from the next room, or from behind a screen.

To those who did manage to meet her in person, the poet was seldom pleasant. Her Aunt Elisabeth, she cackled, was "the only male relative on the female side." An elderly lady looking for lodging was directed to the local cemetery—"to spare," Dickinson explained, "expense of moving." And literary adviser Thomas Higginson, who may or may not have had something of a mash on his protégée, nonetheless found her oddly overbearing. "I never was with any one who drained my nerve power so much," he wrote.

Not that there was much chance of that. *Husband* was the one word which gave the otherwise-articulate genius the fits. Sniped lifelong friend Helen Hunt Jackson in a letter: " 'The man I live with' (I suppose you recollect designating my husband by that curiously direct phrase) is in New York." Nonetheless, it was apparent that an ardent heart beat beneath Ms. Dickinson's chaste white frock. "Wild Nights— Wild Nights!" began one untitled poem penned by the then-thirtyish spinster. "Were I with thee / Wild Nights should be / our luxury!" Subsequent scholars never could agree as to precisely whom that theoretical "thee" was supposed to be—nor even on the gender of the person upon whom Dickinson bestowed her putative passion.

Literally speaking, however, the point was moot: Even Judge Otis P. Lord, the main man in Dickinson's life, could not persuade his poet to engage in any of those exuberant evenings in a less literary context. Though ostensibly madly in love, descending from the heady heights of her solitude into the mundane morass of matrimony was just another one of those things she simply would not do. "Don't you know you are happiest while I withhold and not confer," she rebuked His Honor, who was presumably in increasing ecstasy as the Emily-less years passed; "Don't you know that 'No' is the wildest word we consign to language?"

THE POETESS DICKINSON

"Assent—and you are sane;
Demure—you're straightway dangerous
And handled with a Chain."

—E. D.

Scarlet Editor

Like her famous mate, Sophia Hawthorne harbored literary ambitions. But though husband Nathaniel praised passages of his wife's writing as "the most perfect pictures that ever were put on paper," he strictly forbade her to publish her work. In the end, silent Sophia had the last word: While preparing her spouse's *American Notebooks* for posthumous publication, she excised real or perceived vulgarities, altered names with a free hand, and embellished the manuscript by inserting her own favorite phrases where possible (and sometimes, it seems, where not).

Louisa May Alcott (1832–1888)
Belittled Women

"I am old for my age, and don't care for girls' thing," thirteen-year-old Louisa May Alcott recorded in her diary. Under the circumstances, the statement was scarcely surprising. The daughter of a penniless Utopian philosopher and an activist mother who ran a shelter for abused wives, it was clear to adolescent Alcott that self-reliance was a virtue and marriage no guarantee of financial or physical security.

The primary breadwinner of her family from the age of eighteen onward, Alcott's earliest economic ventures were confined to the sort considered most suitable for her sex—governess, maid, seamstress, schoolteacher, and so on. And even when she began to write, money—not art—was her motive. "Whatever suits the customer," shrugged the pragmatic penswoman. She went on to please her public (and permanently paralyze her thumb) by churning out numerous novels, dozens of potboilers and short stories, and a diary of her experiences as a Civil War nurse.

Left to her own literary devices, Alcott found it most lucrative to pander to popular taste with romantic tales of doomed love and twisted revenge. But in 1868, under strict orders from her publisher to write "a girl's book," she reluctantly turned her talents to the topic of young ladyhood. "I don't enjoy this sort of thing," she complained in her journal. "Never liked girls or knew many, except my sisters; but our queer plays and experiences may prove interesting, though I doubt it." ("Good joke," she would later annotate that particular entry, after the phenomenal success of *Little Women*.) But though profits from her "girl's book" finally assured her family's financial security, Alcott grumbled all the way to the bank, terming *Little Women* and subsequent serials "moral pap for the young."

"Work is my salvation."
—L. M. A.

THE WILDLY SUCCESSFUL LOUISA MAY ALCOTT
LOATHED HER FAMOUS BOOK

Nor did she hold her admiring adolescent audience in high esteem. "Girls write to ask who the little women marry, as if that was the only end and aim of a woman's life," sighed the type-A author, who had no time (and less inclination) for real-life romance. "I *won't* marry Jo to Laurie to please anyone." But in the end, the customer was right once again: in the sequel *Little Men*, her heroine's independence was sacrificed at the altar of Alcott's bankbook and the beloved tomboy became a bride. (Fortunately for poor Jo, she at least wound up with brainy Professor Bhaer, rather than the vacuous boy next door.) But Alcott, who gave the telling title "Happy Women" to an 1868 article singing the praises of independent spinsterhood, never made the mistake of confusing her own life with literature. "I'd rather be a free spirit," wrote the autonomous author, "and paddle my own canoe."

Jessie Frémont (1824–1902)
Behind Every Not-So-Great Man

As far as Jessie (née Benton) Frémont could tell, guys got to have all the fun—and, it seems, most of the glory as well. Her papa was horrified when she cropped her curls and announced that she planned to become a scholar: "Men like their womenkind to be pretty and not of the short-haired variety," she discovered. Relatives pronounced her behavior "scandalous" when she swapped her gown for the garb of a similarly sized male cousin; misses, she was informed, simply did not masquerade as West Point cadets. Her family soundly scolded her for pursuing unsuitable John Frémont, a surveyor not only twelve years her senior, but also quite literally a bastard. And when at seventeen she defiantly married him anyway, her father quit speaking to her altogether.

But by 1842, Mrs. Frémont was leading a more conventionally feminine life in the shadow of her suddenly famous spouse. Not only had John managed to earn a name for himself as an explorer, but he was also achieving recognition as a writer, painting detailed prose portraits of the pristine beauty of California and the Northwest in his reports to the US government. "More than any other work of its time," one historian was to note, "it dramatized the West and made it both alluring and accessible to a generation of restless Americans."

But the writing was unique for another reason. Unknown to Mr. Frémont's fans, it was actually penned by his talented wife—who had never traveled farther west than St. Louis. "I write more easily by dictation," her husband explained. He also wrote more easily, it seems, when someone else thought up the words for him. And though the reports were submitted in Jessie's hand, it never occurred to anyone that they were not actually composed by the man who signed his name. "Simple, clear, unassuming, beautifully graphic," gushed the Washington Union. "Seldom paralleled in the annals of adventure," added the *Democratic Review*, "and never surpassed by anything we have read."

During the course of her life, the gifted ghostwriter never received credit for her contribution to westward migration. She did, however, score a personal triumph during the presidential campaign of 1856, when it became clear that many voters preferred her to Mr. Frémont, the Republican nominee. "Jessie for the White House," read one banner in New Hampshire. "What a shame *women* can't vote!" lamented feminist Lydia Child; "We'd carry 'our Jessie' into the White House, *wouldn't* we." Neither Jessie nor John, of course, was to win the election; that distinction would go to James Buchanan. Fired from his government post in 1861, the unsuccessful Mr. Frémont proceeded to further distinguish himself by losing the family fortune through speculation proceeded to further distinguish himself by losing the family fortune through speculation in railroad stocks. The only fully functional wage-earner of the family, his wife had little choice but to fall back on her writing skills, compiling four memoirs and turning out several articles for the *Atlantic Monthly* and *Harper's* during the 1870s and 1880s. This time around, however, the glory (not to mention the byline) was all her own.

"I am like a deeply built ship. I drive best under a stormy wind."

—J. F.

CONTROVERSIAL CURERS AND INGENIOUS INVALIDS

Elizabeth Blackwell (1821–1910)
Alone in Her Class

Historically speaking, it has generally been deemed more appropriate for ladies to marry MDs than to earn them. But brilliant Elizabeth Blackwell, the first American woman to obtain a medical degree, wasn't interested in shackling herself to a spouse. Indeed, her primary reason for pursuing a medical career—or so she claimed—was to place "a strong barrier" between herself and the stultifying bonds of matrimony. By the mid-1840s, however, Blackwell's unique strategy for spinsterhood was beginning to appear somewhat ill-conceived; in addition to several marriage proposals, she had collected twenty-nine rejection letters from medical schools. To their rather dubious credit, a few relatively enlightened institutions suggested she'd stand a fighting chance if she changed her name and started dressing in the masculine mode. But in 1847, tiny Geneva College in upstate New York finally voted to admit the aspiring female physician, petticoats and all. Unfortunately, it did so under the erroneous belief that her application was a joke.

Amid jeers and catcalls, the all-male student body of that obscure institution had passed a tongue-in-cheek resolution that "to every branch of scientific education, the door should be open equally to all," and formally invited the supposedly fictitious Miss Blackwell to join them in the noblest of human pursuits. Needless to say, the future doctors of America were startled out of their skins when their new and conspicuously contoured classmate sauntered into anatomy class, mid-dissection, as though she had a perfect right to be there. "Some of the students blushed," Blackwell recorded in her journal; "some were hysterical, not one could keep in a smile, and some...held down their faces and shook." Nor did the good citizens of Geneva see fit to extend even the most cursory of small-town courtesies. "As I walked backward and forward to college, the ladies stopped to stare at me," reported Blackwell, "as at a curious animal." It was, she soon discovered, the prevailing theory that "I was a bad woman, whose designs would gradually become evident, or that, being insane, an outbreak of insanity would soon be apparent."

Much to the disappointment of those who expected a more dramatic denouement, Blackwell distinguished herself at Geneva College solely by dint of academic accomplishment, graduating at the top of her class in 1849. But though a crowd of twenty thousand (which no doubt numbered a few sincere supporters among the hordes of curiosity-seekers) turned out to see her receive her diploma, the school was never again to repeat its inadvertent experiment in coeducation, and Blackwell remained the solitary alumna. Sighed the nation's only female MD: "I understand why this life has never been lived before. It *is* hard, with no support but a high purpose, to live against every species of social opposition."

THE GOOD DOCTOR

"I should like a little fun now and then.
Life is altogether too sober."

—E. B.

A Religious Foundation

What is it about Christians and carpentry? During her forty-six-year tenure in the heathen Oregon territory, Mother Joseph of Montreal's Sisters of Providence not only drew up blueprints for more than thirty public buildings, but literally helped lay their foundations. It remains a matter of conjecture whether this God-fearing forewoman went on to reap a suitable eternal reward for her labors. But in 1952, half a century after her death, the American Institute of Architects bestowed its own belated blessing on the mortar-mixing missionary, naming her "the Pacific Northwest's first architect."

Lydia Pinkham (1819–1883)
Queen of Quacks

Would menstrual madness never cease? Everywhere one turned, crampish ladies were lying down with the Victorian vapors—or worse yet, rising up with bloody hatchets in their hands. Indeed, patent medicine magnate Lydia E. Pinkham wanted the world to know, one Connecticut clergyman had actually been killed by his wigged-out wife, her "insanity brought on by sixteen years of suffering with Female Complaints the cause." This tasteless tragedy, Ms. Pinkham hastened to add, might easily have been averted: "Lydia E. Pinkham's Vegetable Compound, the sure cure for these complaints, would have prevented the direful deed." Unlike that homicidal antiheroine, however, Pinkham had more cause to celebrate than curse the phenomenon of PMS. Trained as a nurse and midwife, the fifty-six-year-old first began hawking her homemade herb medicine in 1875 when the family finances took a precipitous nosedive in the stock market. (Reluctant to deposit all her ova in one basket, she also bolstered the bank account by charging her four grown sons for room, board, and personal expenses.) It was not, to say the least, a period known for candid discussions of garden-variety gynecological complaints, let alone infertility, fibroid tumors, and prolapsed uteri—all of which Pinkham claimed her Compound could cure. Nor, in that day, did modest Massachusetts matrons plaster their photographs on products circulated nationwide. Nonetheless, soaring sales indicated that women found Pinkham's grandmotherly countenance ("the best-known American female face of the nineteenth century," according to one historian) soothing rather than shocking, and her claims plausible rather than pathetic. By 1883, the frankly female enterprise was grossing $300,000 annually; even after Pinkham's death, company revenues (now controlled by her sons) would continue to rise, peaking at $3.8 million in 1925.

Pharmacologically speaking, the rather poetic contents of the Compound (unicorn root, fenugreek, and black cohosh) probably didn't pack much of a medicinal wallop. On the other hand, the product *was* guaranteed to bring temporary relief: the maven of menstruation laced her roily concoction with enough alcohol to render it a euphoric forty proof. Oddly enough, this last ingredient was studiously overlooked by the high-minded ladies of the Women's Christian Temperance Union, many of whom offered the peculiar pick-me-up their most enthusiastic endorsement.

But if Pinkham's product wasn't, as she insisted, "The Greatest Medical Discovery Since the Dawn of History," that spirited precursor to Midol probably did save some lives. in 1876, the same year the Vegetable Compound was patented, a prominent American physician was urging the removal of healthy ovaries as a surefire treatment for cramps. Across the board, women who consulted male medics for periodic pain usually wound up on the operating table, where the mortality rate ran as high as 40 percent. Under the circumstances, an ounce of copacetic Vegetable Compound was far preferable to a pound of all-too-permanent cure.

> "Trust Lydia Pinkham, not the doctor who doesn't understand your problems."
>
> —L. P.

Bethenia Owens (1840–1926)
Dreaded Doctor

At the age of thirty-one, milliner Bethenia Owens decided to try on a different type of chapeau. "But I was not prepared," admitted the resident of Roseburg, Oregon, "for the storm of opposition that followed. My family felt they were being disgraced...people sneered and laughed derisively." From her description, one might imagine that Owens—already stigmatized by the scandal of divorce—had decided to pursue a career as a streetwalker or possibly as a hired assassin. But in fact, her controversial decision was merely to become a doctor.

"I always did think you were a smart woman, but you must have lost your senses and gone stark crazy," remarked one of her more supportive acquaintances. "You will change your mind when I come back as a physician," shot back the would-be MD, "and charge you more than I ever have for your hats and bonnets." Her unfortunate experiences at the Eclectic School of Medicine in Philadelphia, however, taught Owens far more about men than medicine: The male students at the teaching hospital hurled rotten eggs at the coeds, and the dean was convicted of selling fraudulent degrees.

Still, the newly (if dubiously) degreed Dr. Owens thought the crisis might have passed when a few formerly scornful Roseburg doctors requested her assistance at an autopsy. But it was a hopeless case. The invitation, it turned out, had been intended as a snub, and her peers actually jeered when she showed up to help carve the corpse. "What is the difference between the attendance of a woman at a male autopsy, and the attendance of a man at a female autopsy? fumed the female physician. But when the morally outraged populace ran her out of town, the answer was all too clear.

Fortunately, the city of Portland harbored no such unhealthy animosity toward doctors in dresses. There Owens conducted a profitable practice for several years, financing her sister's college education and her son's medical training. Still, her own inferior preparation for her profession continued to rankle. "I have done my duty to those depending on me," declared the upwardly mobile medic in 1878, "and now I will treat myself to a full medical course." So at the age of forty-one, Owens took her second degree from the eminently respectable Michigan Medical College, specializing in diseases of the eye and ear.

Just as she had suspected, there was much work to be done in that field. Returning from a tour of European hospitals in 1881, Owens found that American customs agents could believe neither their eyes nor their ears when she declared that she was a doctor. Not until she presented her credentials was permission grudgingly granted to pass her medical instruments duty-free into the country. Obviously, the day had not yet come when a medical degree would be deemed any sort of feather in a female cap. Nonetheless, the ex-milliner's prognosis for progress remained guardedly optimistic. "Time will tell," she predicted; "People have been known to change their minds."

> "The regret of my life up to the age of thirty-five was that I had not been born a boy, for I realized very early in life that a girl was hampered and hemmed in on all sides simply by the accident of sex."
>
> —B. O.

A Patently Obvious Solution

No lady likes to see the remnants of her beau's breakfast riding on his handlebar moustache. In 1899, inventor May Evans did her bit to beautify America by creating a "moustache-guard for attachment to spoons or cups when used in the act of eating soup and other liquids food or drinking coffee." The world is still waiting, however, for the invention that reminds absentminded to lower the toilet seat.

Phoebe Pember (1823–1913)
Nasty Nurse

Brainy Phoebe Pember thought it only natural that the surgeon-in-chief of the Confederate Army had "wisely...decided to have an educated and efficient woman at the head of his hospital." But in 1862, when the thirty-nine-year-old widow was appointed head matron of the huge Chimborazo military hospital in Richmond, Virginia, most male minds recoiled from the thought of a person in petticoats infiltrating the manly medical domain. As Pember would later write in her autobiographical *A Southern Woman's Story*, the shocking word soon went around the facility that "*one of them had come.*"

Contrary to all expectations, however, the able administrator took a decidedly virile approach to the care and feeding of the seventy-six thousand patients who passed through Chimborazo during the course of the Civil War. "Why man! The very babies of the Confederacy have given up drinking milk, and here you are, six feet two, crying for it," she scolded one malingering malcontent. Bandaging bloody wounds was a cinch for the Georgia belle; ever so calmly, she ushered many a moribund male toward his ultimate destiny. And to the disappointment of her detractors, not once did she swoon at the sight of anatomical regions which the truly refined rebel rarely encountered in the course of civilian life.

Despite her distinguished performance, however, numerous unenlightened gentlemen harbored a distinctly unhealthy attitude toward the unflappable female. One ill-mannered invalid—a "rough-looking Texan"—circled the minute matron for several minutes, staring "till I supposed some progenitor of his family had been an owl." (Snapped a peevish Pember: "Did you never see a woman before?") And when she decreed that certain dipsomaniac doctors would no longer enjoy access to the anesthetizing whiskey barrel, a virulent epidemic of hostility raged through the hospital corridors.

Aware that a scalpel-sharp tongue alone would not always shield her from the slings and arrows of anti-female prejudice, Pember secretly augmented her arsenal of administrative weapons. Just as she had foreseen, her "little friend," as she termed the pistol she carried in her breast pocket, proved itself invaluable when a drunken soldier stormed into her quarters late one night. Seizing the strong-willed superintendent by the shoulder, he announced that he had come to collect the coveted whiskey barrel. And when she refused to yield, he let slip "a name that a decent woman seldom hears and even a wicked one resents." That did it. Out came the gun, which Pember held firm against the ear of the half-looped lout. "You had better leave," she hissed, "for if *one* bullet is lost, there are five more ready, and the room is too small for even a woman to miss six times."

The soused sexist departed in haste, leaving Pember to register another victory—and another mortal enemy—on the chart of her Chimborazo career. Just as the horrified staff had shuddered on her arrival, one of "them" *had* come—and bitter as that pill might prove, it was one they would nevertheless have to swallow.

"In the midst of suffering and death...a woman must soar beyond the conventional modesty considered correct under different circumstances."

—P. P.

Treat Her Like a Lady

According to one calico-bonnetted bride of 1875, a good man wasn't so hard to find on the Western frontier. "Guess my husband's got to look after me, and make himself agreeable to me, if he can," she explained to William Dixon, a visiting Englishman; "If he don't, there's plenty will."

Charlotte Perkins Gilman (1860–1935)
The Handwriting on the Wallpaper

"Lie down an hour after each meal," a famous Philadelphia neurologist advised writer Charlotte Perkins Gilman, who was suffering from marital malaise and a deep-seated desire not to clean the house. "Have but two hours intellectual life a day. And never touch pen, brush, or pencil as long as you live." Unfortunately, that curious counsel was no anomaly in 1885; doctors routinely dispensed an admonition against activity to women afflicted with "nervous prostration," a condition thought to stem from overstimulation of the fragile female nervous system. Rest and relaxation in the bosom of the family constituted the state-of-the-art cure. But Gilman, whose nerves were already "wilted" and whose mind resembled "a piece of boiled spinach," thought the physician's suggestion sounded more like a recipe for turning into vegetable soup.

"Life is a verb!" she would later write. "Life consists of action." So leaving her spouse to cope with the dirty dishes, Gilman fled to California and proceeded to pen her own alternative prescription for well-being. Flexing those forbidden mental muscles, she discovered the "joy and growth" that had eluded her as a pampered Victorian pet. Flouting the taboo against hard work, she reclaimed the "measure of power" denied to those who devoted their lives to passive pedestal adornment. And in her internationally acclaimed *Women and Economics*, which traced a plethora of social ills to suffocating marriages, Gilman recommended a thoroughly rigorous route to recovery for ladies languishing in their gilded cages.

Nowhere, however, did the self-healed heroine so eloquently state her case against the stifling status quo as in "The Yellow Wallpaper," her 1892 story of a conventional housewife's descent into insanity. But like the male medic who had misdiagnosed the writer's malady, not every reader was capable of comprehending the nature of an unhappy woman's private hell. Indeed, vivid descriptions of "strangled heads and bulbous eyes and waddling fungus" provoked one American anthologizer to relegate the piece to the horror genre. "Such a story," asserted another disgusted student of literature, "ought not to be written. It was enough to drive anyone mad to read it." But Gilman knew better—and so, a century later, do contemporary readers who heed the caveat of that chilling tale. According to the author, the only story that could truly drive a woman insane was her own autobiography, written in the passive voice.

"To the boy, we say 'Do'; to the girl, 'Don't.'"

—C. P. G.

Alice James (1848-1892)
A Sickening Story

What was a girl to do? The really nifty careers, as Alice James couldn't help noting, had already been nabbed by her brothers: Henry enjoyed a reputation as the nation's most accomplished novelist, William as its foremost psychologist. Matrimony—"the only successful occupation that a woman can undertake"—just wasn't the sensitive little sister's cup of tea. Men, she shuddered, "have got about as much manners and civilization as gorillas." Under the circumstances, there appeared to be nothing Ms. James could do—and nothing was precisely what she did during her lifelong career of languishing in bed. To her credit, however, she did it exceptionally well, transforming her boudoir into the forum for her own offbeat brand of Jamesian brilliance.

Diagnosed variously as suffering from neurasthenia, neuralgia, nervous hyperesthenia, and the ever-fashionable hysteria, James' ill-defined ailments were a never-ending source of interest to Boston's most intellectually distinguished family. "The truth is that we are so wholly immersed in Alice' malady," confessed her father, "that we are apt to think there is no one else sick and suffering in the world."

Far from feeling oppressed by the familial obsession with her fragility, the accomplished invalid deemed it the only healthy state of affairs. "If you don't come soon," she wrote to one neglectful friend, "I shall in desperation elope with the handsome butcher-boy." When cruel William transferred his attentions toward another woman in 1878, Alice James eclipsed the announcement of his engagement by collapsing in hysteria—or was it nervous hyperesthenia?—and declaring herself too ill to attend the nuptials. ("It seems rather inconsiderate of William," agreed ever-obliging Henry, "to have selected such a moment for making merry.") Nor was she above playing the emotional tyrant's trump card, pointedly inquiring of her father if he "thought that suicide...was a sin." Having duly received parental permission "to end her life whenever she pleased," however, Alice James evidently found the option considerably less attractive.

Every career, even the most ignoble, eventually achieves a pinnacle of some sort; James' moment came in 1891. "Ever since I have been ill, I have longed and longed for some palpable disease," she exulted in her diary; "To him who waits, all things come!" To most, the occasion for her glee—a diagnosis of terminal breast cancer—would have come as a shock and a tragedy. But to the chronic invalid, it was the pièce de résistance in her collection of medical complaints—the ultimate crowning triumph.

> "I was born bad and I never have recovered."
>
> —A. J.

Red Badge of Courage

According to adrenaline addict Clara Barton, nursing in the Civil War era was no profession for the namby-pamby. In the course of her medical career, the valiant volunteer dodged Minnie balls, performed ad hoc surgery with her pocket knife, and once had to wring "the blood from the bottom of my clothing before I could step, for the weight about my feet." Justifiably proud of her contribution to the Union, Barton went on to reiterate her resume at a congressional banquet in 1892—at length, and in verse. "She stanches his blood, cools the fever-burnt breath, / And the wave of her hand stays the Angel of Death," declaimed the patriot-turned-poet...and so on. Fortunately, fate is not always as cruel as critics: Just as she deserved, bold Ms. Barton is remembered today chiefly for her role in founding the American Red Cross—and not for her bloody awful poetry.

CLARA BARTON

Catherine Beecher (1800–1878)
Bathing Beauty

At first blush, it was difficult to imagine stiff-spined Catherine Beecher cavorting at a bathing spa. It was not the prim schoolteacher, after all, but her sister Harriet Beecher Stowe who once declared, "I won't be any properer than I've a mind to be." The model of Victorian propriety, conventional Catherine couldn't even bring herself to deliver her own lectures on pedagogy. Instead, she prevailed upon brother Henry Ward to speak while she sat in sphinx-like silence, secure in the conviction that ladies, like children, should be seen and not heard. And, the self-acknowledged antisuffragist freely admitted, the frank aim of her Western Female Institute in Oxford, Ohio, was to whip girls into shape for their only proper role in life—that of wives and mothers. (That she herself was neither never appeared to trouble her.)

But in the popular East Coast resorts known as "water cures," the stern schoolmarm had no qualms about letting it all hang out.

Ostensibly, Beecher's interest in tub therapy was purely medical: She suffered from a chronic condition to which she gave the name "nervous excitability." Precisely how this peculiar affliction manifested itself is not entirely clear; interestingly enough, however, the purported remedy consisted largely of taking cold showers. In any event, Beecher found the water cure of "inestimable benefit" in improving not only her health, but also, it seems, her social life.

Beecher's first water cure companion appears to have been professional peer Nancy Johnson, whom she treated to an all-expenses-paid session at a Brattleboro resort in 1846. Just as promised, Johnson found the experience beneficial. By the end of the excursion, she had landed a job as Beecher's "personal secretary," presumably with all the concomitant rights and responsibilities. Next in the string of spa sisters came scholar Delia Bacon, who scored an invitation to join Beecher for a month at the Round Hill Water Cure in Northampton. Again, the investment paid off—for three years, the bathing buddies were known as constant companions. And when Bacon left Beecher high and dry, Beecher took up the slack with one Mary Mortimer, splashing through another Round Hill season in her company. Ms. Mortimer too proved an accommodating pool pal, and she was subsequently rewarded with a post at Beecher's school.

Only truly indecorous minds will venture to conjecture whether any of these bathhouse conquests ever escalated into steamy passion, or instead consisted exclusively of those intense platonic relationships known at the time (in whatever geographical zone they transpired) as Boston marriages. As to the real allure of the water cure, however, it should be noted that Beecher continued to make frequent trips to Brattleboro and Round Hill long after she had accepted her "nervous excitability" as a permanent and unalterable condition.

"A woman who has tolerable health finds herself so much above the great mass of her friends...that she feels herself a prodigy of good health."

—C. B.

The Depreciated Damsel

Entirely too late, young Alma de Bretteville of San Francisco learned that her good-time Charlie wasn't the marrying kind. But the vindictive ex-virgin didn't take the blow lying down. "I sued for personal defloweration," she later recalled, "and by God, I won." Well, yes and no. it seems that de Bretteville, who periodically posed unclothed for local artists, valued her maidenhood at $50,000. The turn-of-the-century jury, however, concluded that a more modest $1,250 should adequately cover the damages.

ALARMINGLY LITIGIOUS LADIES

Ah Toy (1828–1928)
Libertines and Justice for All

In the annals of American legal history, it is the rare courtesan indeed who enters a courtroom entirely of her own volition. But to ambitious Ah Toy, a Cantonese call girl whose arrival in San Francisco coincided—not entirely accidentally—with that of a plethora of profligate miner forty-niners, "justice for all" was more than a pretty phrase. In 1849, the democratically minded demimondaine made her debut as a plaintiff before Judge George Baker of the San Francisco Recorder's Court.

Resplendent in an apricot satin jacket and willow green pantaloons, the miffed Ms. Toy charged several clients (including more than one prominent pillar of the community) with failure to make appropriate compensation for services rendered. As to the specific nature of her business, she was somewhat less forthcoming. Gentlemen called upon her—or so one reporter delicately translated her testimony—"to gaze upon the countenance of the charming Ah Toy." (Fortunately for the coy Cyprian, Judge Baker evidently chose to interpret this odd explanation as an elegant euphemism rather than a brazen act of perjury.) In any event, Toy continued, her customary exhibition fee was one ounce in gold, weighed out on her own set of scales. Recently, however, certain cheapskate countenance-gazers had taken to passing off less precious metals as the genuine ore. And here the well-prepared plaintiff triumphantly produced her cold hard evidence: a china basin brimming with brass filings.

Though both case and courtesan were eventually thrown out of court, Toy would seek redress for grievances on at least two subsequent occasions. In 1851, she filed charges against a light-fingered lover who, reported one local paper, "after politely visiting her house and taking a drink with her," had boorishly boosted a diamond brooch. And in 1952, she appeared as counsel for a colleague seeking to recover so-called "debts of honor."

As time went by, however, the scales of justice were less often to tip in Toy's favor. Prosecuted with increasing vigor for practicing her profession, the libidinous litigant was arrested and fined several times between 1854 and 1859 before she was finally routed from the red-light district in 1860. In a freewheeling boomtown teeming with scarlet sisters and boisterous bachelors, one could scarcely argue that Toy's trade affronted the rather lax prevailing standards of decency. Like many an idealistic immigrant, however, she was clearly guilty of mistaking democratic rhetoric for reality. As to whether the pursuit of justice will ever truly be a worthwhile pastime for those who are neither male nor pale, nor conventionally moral, history will have to stand as judge.

"Men are generally more law-abiding than women. Women have the feeling that since they didn't make the rules, the rules have nothing to do with them."

—Diane Johnson

Clara Foltz (1849–1934)
Right vs. Might

Passing the California bar was the least of the trials of aspiring attorney Clara Foltz. "A woman's place is at home, unless it is as a teacher," chided one prominent San Jose lawyer, who perhaps did not relish the prospect of a clever competitor encroaching on his high-income turf. "If you would like a position in our public schools, I will be glad to recommend you."

As a financially strapped divorcée, however, Foltz was more interested in feeding her own five children than in educating the progeny of other mothers. But in 1878, California still reserved the lucrative privilege of practicing law for "any white male citizen." Proving the premise of that sexist statute a lie, the stubborn single mother took it upon herself to draft a more democratic amendment. She prevailed upon a state legislator to sponsor the controversial new "Woman Lawyer's Bill."

"Narrow-gauge statesmen grew as red as turkey gobblers mouthing their ignorance against the bill," she later recalled. Inevitably, there were impassioned arguments that "lady lawyers were dangerous to justice inasmuch as an impartial jury would be impossible when a lovely woman pleaded the cases of a criminal." Nonetheless, the measure squeaked through by a margin of two votes, and Foltz—the first female admitted to the California bar—was soon doing a brisk business in the burgeoning divorce trade. Nor was her triumph tainted by die-hard chauvinists who still insisted that the only proper female profession was bringing up babies. "A woman had better be in almost any business than raising such men as you," retorted the successful new solicitor.

Evidently an unusually conscientious counselor, Foltz enrolled in Hastings Law School in San Francisco late in 1878 to fill the gaps in her self-administered legal education. Her tenure as a student, however, was short-lived. "The first day," she recalled, "I had a bad cold and was forced to cough. To my astonishment, every young man in the class was seized with a violent fit of coughing." Three lectures later, Hastings summarily booted out the indignant barrister, asserting the right to refuse admission to those whose presence would be "useless to such persons themselves...or interfere with the proper discipline and instruction of the students." California courts, however, sided with the lady lawyer (who, it was reported, presented her case "with both force and polish), and she was eventually permitted to pursue her JD.

Ironically, however, Foltz never received the diploma that was her legal due: A flourishing practice soon precluded further formal study. As for her ill-behaved classmates, "They must have been an inferior lot," she smirked, "for certain it is, I have never seen nor heard tell of one of them from that day to this."

"The story of my triumphs will eventually disclose that though the battle has been long and hard-fought, it was worthwhile."

—C. F.

Belva Lockwood (1830–1917)
Precedential Material

In 1876, when forty-six-year-old Belva Lockwood was denied permission to practice before the US Court of Claims, the august Justice Drake found it necessary to explain the facts of life to her. "Mistress Lockwood, you are a woman," he pointed out. It was not the first time that the Washington, DC, attorney had been apprised of that interesting bit of information: Five years previously, several law schools had rejected her application on that basis, one nothing that "the attendance of ladies would be an injurious diversion of the attention of the students."

It was, however, the first occasion on which the United States found itself sued by a female lawyer who, despite the "amazement and dismay" of "nine gowned judges," planned to practice law in the highest courts in the nation. And in 1879, after a fierce five-year battle with Congress to pass a bill guaranteeing that no citizen would "be excluded as an attorney…from any court of the United States on account of sex," the persistent plaintiff became the first woman sworn in by both the Supreme Court and the Court of Claims. Not content to rest on her legal laurels, Ms. Lockwood went on to stun Washington by opening a mother-daughter law firm, winning a five million dollar settlement against the government for the Cherokee Nation, and treating the town to glimpses of her scarlet stockings as she pedaled to work on her three-wheeler.

By 1884, Belva's gender had apparently slipped her mind once again: She announced herself as a candidate for the US presidency on the ticket of the tiny National Equal Rights party. An anomaly in every way, the Lockwood presidential package included not only a platform calling for "universal peace," but would-be VP Marietta Stow, founder of a controversial California health regimen known as "Cold Food."

Nevertheless, the pair professed astonishing confidence in their popularity: "The Nation's heart beats in unison with the Equal-Rights party," opined optimistic Stow. (Besides, she pointed out, a fifty-four-year-old female would certainly "bring no blush or barnacles of youthful, or *mature*, 'wild oats sowing' into the White House.")

As it turned out, the Nation's heart was smitten by Democrat Grover Cleveland and did not consider Lockwood a serious rival for its affections. But the all-male Belva Lockwood club in New Jersey, for one, vastly enjoyed her campaign and took to sporting Mother Hubbard dresses, bonnets, and parasols in parody of the controversial candidate. Numerous suffragists, however, were not so amused: "The damage done by her and a little band of eccentric zealots in California," sniffed one feminist journal, "cannot be estimated." And, some suggested, the sole purpose of Lockwood's bid for office was to attract attention to herself, thereby increasing patronage of her law practice.

But Lockwood—who did manage to garner 4,149 votes and the entire electoral vote of Indiana—never regretted her decision and went on to repeat the experiment, though with less success, in 1888. "We shall never have rights until we take them, or respect until we command it," she wrote. And, she added—for once not waiting for someone else to bring up the subject of her sex—"My cause was the cause of thousands of women."

INSTEAD WE ELECTED THIS GUY, WHO MARRIED HIS
FRIEND'S DAUGHTER. HE WAS FORTY-NINE,
SHE TWENTY-ONE.

"Reforms are slow, but they never go backward."

—B. L.

OUTRAGEOUS ORATORS AND SASSY SUFFRAGISTS

Sojourner Truth (1797–1883)
Frankly Feminine

Former slave and abolitionist orator Sojourner Truth was touted by an admiring Harriet Beecher Stowe as "the Libyan Sibyl." In point of fact, the self-named speaker hailed from upstate New York, and the first language that rolled off her tongue was European rather than African, the legacy of a Dutch slaveowner. But at least Stowe got her gender right. To those who believed that no bona fide female—let alone one born into bondage—would make so bold as to speak in public, the issue was evidently open to debate.

"Sojourner Truth," reported the *St. Louis Dispatch*, "is the name of a man now lecturing in Kansas City." In Silver Lake, Indiana, an audience amused itself by voting on the question, and a committee of matrons convened to examine her bosom. The opportunity was not lost on Truth, who described to her prurient public how she had been forced to nurse white children against her will, when she could have been nursing her own. At the conclusion of her remarks, she ripped open her bodice, baring her well-used breasts to all. "See for yourselves!" she sneered. "Do you wish also to suck?"

To one clergyman at the Akron women's rights convention in 1851, however, even a positively IDed bosom was no proof of womanhood. Arguing against suffrage, he painted the classic Victorian portrait of upper-crust feminine fragility: Ladies would, in essence, succumb to the vapors when exposed to the rigors of the voting booth. And as

Truth—no delicate Mayflower daughter, but a large, imposing woman in her fifties—rose to respond, "a hissing sound of disapprobation" (or so reported chairwoman Frances Gage) echoed through the room.

But Truth would not be silenced. "That man over there says that women need to be helped into carriages, and lifted over ditches, and to have the best places everywhere," she exploded. "Nobody ever helps me into carriages, or over mud-puddles, or gives me any best place! And aren't I a woman?" (Here she bared her right arm to the shoulder, revealing powerful biceps resulting from years of hard labor.) "I could work as much and eat as much as a man—when I could get it—and bear the lash as well! And aren't I a woman? I have borne thirteen children, and seen them most all sold off to slavery, and when I cried out with my mother's grief, none but Jesus heard me! And aren't I a woman?"

That eloquent equal rights manifesto would of course go down as a classic in both abolitionist and feminist history. But though Truth had proven herself to Akron, she had not borne the final blow in her struggle for recognition as a Black, female human being. In Missouri, she was mobbed for speaking her mind; in Kansas, she was clubbed. And in Washington during the Civil War, a streetcar conductor slammed her against the door when she attempted to step onto the coach. "Stand back, n****r, and let that lady on," he snarled. But Truth boarded anyway, and rode, upright and uncompromising, to the end of the line. After all, she reasoned, "I am a lady too."

"If the first woman God ever made was strong enough to turn the world upside down all alone, these women together ought to be able to turn it back and get it right side up."

—S. T.

A REAL WOMAN

Anna Shaw (1847–1919)

Self-Conscious Clergywoman

In the 1860s, delicate damsels laced tight and fainted with abandon; an artful swoon, it was felt, was the hallmark of femininity. But after aspiring minister Anna Shaw did the ladylike thing during a speech to her high school elocution class, she resolved never to so disgrace herself again. No fragile flower, the Michigan homesteader's daughter was more accustomed to felling trees in the Michigan forest than falling to the floor. Besides, for a potential preacher, passing out on the platform was a serious professional liability. "If I let that failure stand against me," she wrote, "I could never more afterward speak in public."

Unfortunately, Shaw's family apparently preferred a comatose daughter to a clergywoman. A truly pious lady, they grumbled, belonged in the pew, not on the pulpit. Soon a startling notice appeared in the local newspaper: "A young girl named Anna Shaw, seventeen years old, preached at Ashton yesterday. Her real friends deprecate the course she is pursuing."

Still more subversive was the approach essayed by another purported pal, who entreated well-known women's rights lecturer Mary Livermore to discourage her friend from a controversial career in the public eye. Veiling her argument in very Victorian terms, she insisted that Shaw lacked sufficient stamina for her self-appointed task; there was a distinct danger, she warned, that her Christian comrade might work herself to death. Fortunately, however, there was no sense preaching old-world values to the newfangled feminist. Responded Livermore, rather briskly: "It is better that she should die doing the things she wants to than that she should die because she can't."

So inspired, Shaw went on to take her divinity degree from Boston University, was ordained as a Methodist minister in 1871, and after an interesting all-night chat with Susan B. Anthony in 1888, devoted the remainder of her life to speaking out against sexism. Audiences across the country warmed to the outspoken orator: A crowd of cowboys at an Oregon rodeo was even moved to present her with a banner bearing the inscription, "Woman Suffrage—We Are All for It." To her "real friends," however, Shaw's success as a speaker only confirmed the wisdom of contemporary etiquette manuals, which inevitably prescribed myriad circumstances under which a lady should make sure she fainted. Evidently a woman who refused to lose consciousness on cue was capable of anything—including raising that of the entire nation.

"Congenial work, no matter how much there
is of it, has never killed anyone."

—A. S.

Mary Lease (1850–1933)
Populist Party Girl

The art of mincing words utterly escaped motormouthed orator Mary Lease. "What you farmers need is to raise less corn and more hell!" thundered the popular proselytizer for the alternative People's Party; "Let the bloodhounds of money who have dogged us thus far beware!" At a different historical moment, needless to say, the denizens of the nation's breadbasket would have taken a dim view of any speechifier in skirts, let alone one who spouted profanities. In the early 1890s, however, mesmerized and mostly male audiences across the Midwest hung on her every word. A former Kansas farm wife and self-educated lawyer, Lease gave voice to the mounting fury of America's agricultural sector, doubly squeezed by governmental policies and foreclosure-happy loan companies.

Foes of the female firebrand, however, found few kind words for a woman whose voice, contrary to Shakespearean caveat, was absolutely never soft, gentle, or low. Proper feminine discussions of domestic policy, they claimed, revolved around dustpans and dishware, not radical reform. "Went to town to hear Joint discussion between Mrs. Lease and John M. Brumbaugh," wrote one appalled audience member; "Poor Brumbaugh was not in it." Sniped another sexist soul, "Her venomous tongue is the only thing marketable about the old harpy. No doubt the petticoated smut-mill earns her money, but few women with any regard for their reputations would care to make their living that way."

Credited as a major contributor to sweeping populist victories in the Kansas elections of 1893, Lease paid little heed to such mean-spirited carping. "My tongue is loose at both ends and hung on a swivel, so I'm likely to have considerable notoriety in the future," she had acknowledged early in her career. Unfortunately, the same double-edged sword that served Lease so well on the stumping circuit was also eventually to sever her ties to the People's Party. Appointed head of the Kansas State Board of Charities in 1894, within the year, she had turned her tart tongue against the populist governor and was fired from her plum post.

In 1896, Lease again provoked the wrath of party leaders when she spoke out against their plan to endorse a Democratic candidate for president. In the midst of her address in a Kansas City convention in that year, an anonymous critic extinguished the lights in the hall, and the lady at the lectern was left shouting into the darkness. Though the nation had not heard the last of the strident stentorian (who went on to campaign for numerous other controversial causes—woman suffrage, prohibition, and birth control among them), that was Lease's final speech on behalf of populism. Just as the sudden symbolic darkness suggested, her moment had passed and it was time for the once-scintillating, now tiresome, life of the People's Party to go home.

> "It is no longer a government of the people, by the people, and for the people, but a government of Wall Street, by Wall Street, and for Wall Street."
>
> —M. L.

Susan B. Anthony (1820–1906)
Sexism and the Single Girl

Sure, Susan B. Anthony didn't have to endure the annoying hubris of a husband. Unshackled by the manacles of matrimony, she was free to think for herself and millions of her disenfranchised sisters. She could come and go as she pleased—so long as the verboten voting booth wasn't her destination. But even for the preeminent strategist of the nineteenth-century women's movement, spinsterhood wasn't one long soiree at Seneca Falls.

"You are not married," chided abolitionist Samuel May as though that fascinating fact might have somehow slipped the busy bachelorette's mind; "You have no business to be discussing marriage." Retorted Anthony, who rather prided herself on the passage of the *Married Women's Property Act*, which gave New York wives control over their own earnings, "You, Mr. May, are not a slave. Suppose you quit lecturing on slavery."

So much for sexist Sam. But why, certain impertinent individuals inquired again and again, wasn't a nice all-American girl like Anthony—a Friend, a farmer's daughter, even a former schoolteacher—spoken for? There was, inevitably, the implication that her passion for patriarchy-smashing derived from a bad case of spinsterish sour grapes and nothing more. In point of fact, the allegedly austere activist didn't lack for beaux, her most significant suitor being a wealthy Quaker from Maine. Simple minds, however, deserved simple answers: Anthony merely snickered that she had no desire to degrade the gentleman she loved by marrying him. Mr. Right, after all, was eligible to vote, own property, and run for the office of president; in good conscience, she couldn't allow him to pledge his allegiance to a political outcast and pariah.

But when it came to the retro assumptions of soul sister Elizabeth Cady Stanton (with Anthony, founder of the National Woman Suffrage Association and coauthor of several volumes of the epic *History of Woman Suffrage*), Susan was at a loss for words. her seven little pre-feminists, Mrs. Stanton pleaded, made it darn difficult to pen the perfect polemic; surely her unencumbered collaborator wouldn't mind doing double duty as an au pair? A preoccupation with hygiene not being prevalent in yesteryear, the nation's most famous babysitter couldn't beg off by claiming she had to cleanse her coiffure. Meekly, Ms. Anthony—the scourge of misogynists from Schenectady to San Francisco—agreed to mind her pal's progeny and may even have been coerced into baking a batch of cookies or two.

A VERY DISTINGUISHED DAYCARE WORKER

Esther Morris (1814–1902)

Territorial Imperative

Like earlier American revolutionaries, Wyoming resident Esther Morris was tired of taxation without representation. She was also tired of not being able to own property in her own name, hold elected office, nor even vote for the candidate of her choice. And like her historical counterparts, she chose to announce her dissatisfaction via the time-honored vehicle of the tea party.

Shortly before Wyoming's first elections in 1869, twenty of the territory's most influential citizens—including two rival candidates for a seat in the legislature—received invitations to the September soiree hosted by the fifty-five-year-old wife of a prospector. As with the nonexistent free lunch, so with that toney tea party: At the crucial moment in the festivities, Morris buttonholed William Bright, the Democratic candidate, and fired the opening salvo in her short and successful equal rights campaign. If elected, she demanded to know, would he introduce a woman suffrage bill? Under the circumstances—his hostess was after all a strapping 180-pound six-footer with a countenance frequently described as "craggy"—Bright quickly discovered his latent enthusiasm for feminism. And during the course of the evening, the Republican candidate too experienced a sudden conversion to the cause.

Acutely aware that the political memory is often a short one, Morris kept up her crusade even after Bright's victory, hounding him mercilessly until he made good on his promise to introduce the "Female Suffrage Act." Needless to say, the unprecedented proposal, which guaranteed the right to vote and hold public office to all Wyoming women over twenty-one years of age, met with no end of sexist snickering. One opponent snidely suggested that the age requirement be changed to thirty, as no member of the fair sex would ever admit to having achieved such an advanced age. Another proposed that the word "women" be stricken and the phrase "colored women and squaws" substituted in its place. But in the end, the bill passed by a significant margin, and the women of Wyoming marched merrily off to the polls—fifty years before Congress approved the national suffrage amendment.

Appropriately enough, Morris, appointed the nation's first female justice of the peace in 1870, was one of the first beneficiaries of the new legislation. Cognizant that her performance would be viewed as a "test of woman's ability to hold public office," she evidently passed the exam with flying colors. During her nine-month term, not one of Morris' seventy judicial decisions was ever reversed on appeal—including a finding against her own husband on charges of assault and battery. Meanwhile, the bemused males of Wyoming continued to propose dubious toasts to the "lovely ladies, once our superiors, now our equals." One imagines, however, that they required something stronger than tea to make that sentiment truly palatable.

"I have assisted in drawing a grand and petit jury, deposited a ballot, and helped canvass the votes after the electing, and performing all these duties, I do not know as I have neglected my family any more than [in] ordinary shopping."

—E. M.

It Wasn't Supposed to End Like This

In 1897, the heroine of Florence Converse's *Diana Victrix* flabbergasted her would-be fiancé (not to mention heterosexual literature lovers across the nation) by informing him that she just wasn't that kind of girl. "Please go away!" she explained. In the first place, she preferred the companionship of her female friend. Besides, she added, "I shouldn't like to keep house and sew… I should hate it!" Reader, she didn't marry him.

Abigail Duniway (1834–1915)
Homely Remedies

From Seneca Falls on down, East Coast suffragists expressed their sentiments by meeting *en masse* and issuing defiant position papers. Some, like Susan B. Anthony, even got themselves arrested to attract attention to the cause. But according to Abigail Duniway—an overworked Oregon housewife who described herself as a "general pioneer drudge," consciousness-raising was more effective than outright confrontation, and honey more effective than vinegar as a medium for catching flies. Flashy "hurrah…and tambourine campaign(s)," she maintained, alienated more supporters than they attracted; it was wiser—though not, of course, nearly so exciting—to work within the system.

At the heart of the Duniway system, as it happened, lay the *New Northwest* journal, a subtly subversive periodical peppered with eye-catching reports on crime and political scandal over which she presided from 1871 to 1887. Those who perused the paper with an eye strictly to the lurid, however, got more than they bargained for: Inevitably, reports of scandalous goings-on were punctuated by the editorial remark that society would be less corrupt were women allowed to vote. But alas, "the virtuous, the refined, the sensible, the noble mothers, wives, and daughters of the nation do not assist in the national housekeeping," Duniway sighed.

Nor was the editor's homely advice to her readers—carefully interspersed with pleasant pieces on coping with corn grubs and constructing waterproof cloaks—designed to perpetuate the status quo. "You need rest," she wrote to "Nervous Sufferer." "Let Molly's face go dirty and John's knee peep out. These things will sure happen when you are dead and gone." Herself a harried homemaker, Duniway didn't need to be told that such homespun propaganda spoke more eloquently than any equal rights manifesto.

On the lecture circuit, too, she doled out a decidedly down-to-earth brand of feminism—perhaps too coarse for East Coast tastes, but perfectly palatable to rural Northwesterners. "I have often known a hen to try to crow, but I've never known one to succeed at it yet," jeered one detractor. "I have myself discovered that peculiarity in hens," responded the plainspoken pioneer; "But...I once saw a rooster try to set, and he made a failure, too."

But though Duniway's decades of writing, lecturing, and lobbying were instrumental in gaining the vote for women in Idaho and Washington, Oregon lagged behind. Eventually, the frustrated National Woman Suffrage Association launched what she bitterly termed an "invasion" of her territory. Just as she had predicted, however, "hurrah and tambourine" tactics were no more successful than her more prosaic form of politics, and the men of Oregon voted down the suffrage amendment year after year until 1912. But as the earthy equal rights enthusiast (at the age of seventy-eight, the first woman to cast her ballot in the state) once informed a sexist skeptic: "I have always though that the difference between a man and a male is that a *man* could change his mind."

"Life's hardest battles everywhere are fought by the others of men in giving existence to the race."

—A. D.

RABBLE ROUSERS AND MUCKRAKERS

Mary Jones, a.k.a. "Mother Jones" (1830–1930)
Mother of Them All

When critics accused Mother Jones of inciting violence, the "most dangerous woman in America" (or so one prosecuting attorney termed her) took it as a compliment. "The militant, not the meek, shall inherit the earth," she proclaimed. A curser, a drinker, a hard-boiled old bird, Jones organized her first labor strike at the age of forty-seven and spent the next forty years roaming the country looking for trouble— and stirring it up when she couldn't find any. In coal and copper mines, in cotton mills and beer breweries, wherever the workingman squirmed beneath the heel of the capitalist oppressor, Mother Jones exhorted him to take up arms—or at least union membership— and rebel. And if she couldn't get the workingman, she'd take his wife instead.

"This is the fighting age," she thundered to a crowd of women in New York City, the sisters and wives of striking streetcar men; "Put on your fighting clothes." So inspired, the ladies proceeded to demolish a car of the New York Railways company using only bricks and their fists as well as inflicting serious damage on several of New York's finest.

In Pennsylvania in 1900, Jones incited a band of anthracite miners' wives to march against nonunion scabs. Armed with the lowly tools of women's work—mops, brooms, and tin pans—they effectively routed the newcomers. One woman, reported the *Washington Post*, "started such a racket by beating her dishpan with a hammer and finally throwing the pan at a mule's head that a stampede started." Soon broomstick brigades were a standard in Jones' repertoire. Sighed one exasperated mine guard: "It is very difficult to deal with women who resort to these tactics."

"Women have been downtrodden," Jones cried; "It is time for them to shake off this vicious hell, to stand up to their full stature and do the work that has been left for them." If her language was a shade more blue, her sentiments echoed exactly those of the most famous feminist figures of the era. But Jones bristled at the suggestion that Susan B. Anthony was her sister. "The plutocrats have organized their women," she scoffed; "They keep them busy with suffrage and prohibition and charity." Blissfully unaware of their abasement, the plutocrats' women kept right on doing their work. But no one who limped home from a battle with the very militant Mother could counter her crowning argument against feminism: "You don't need a vote to raise hell!"

> "Pray for the dead and fight like hell for the living."
> —M. J.

Ida Wells (1862–1931)
A Different Sort of Dreamer

Unlike Angela Davis, anti-racism activist Ida Wells never made the FBI's ten most wanted list. But a good eighty years before Ms. Davis achieved national notoriety, Wells was packing a pistol and urging her sons to "meet fisticuffs with fisticuffs." "I felt that one had better die fighting against injustice," she declared, "than to die like a dog or a rat in a trap."

The twenty-two-year-old Memphis schoolteacher struck her first blow against oppression in 1884, when officials of the recently segregated Chesapeake & Ohio Railroad attempted to oust her from the first-class coach. But the courageous commuter did not go gentle into the smoking car: She clung fast to her seat, bit the conductor, and eventually filed a successful discrimination suit in circuit court. Her triumph, however, proved as transitory as the toothmarks in the railman's flesh in 1887, the Tennessee supreme court overturned the decision, clearing Chesapeake & Ohio of all charges.

Five years later, when Memphis was rocked by the lynching of three Black businessmen, a sadder-but-wiser Wells didn't even think about seeking legal redress. "There is only one thing left that we can do," she asserted in an incendiary article for the *Memphis Free Speech*, "save our money and leave a town which...takes us out and murders us in cold blood when accused by white persons." In response, an estimated six thousand African Americans fled the city, nearly bankrupting the local streetcar company and causing white housewives to deplore the sudden shortage of domestic help.

Not content merely to deplete the pool of maids in Memphis, Wells continued to raise the hackles of hard-core racists—and elevate the consciousness of a few—with *A Red Record*, her 1895 of three years of Southern lynchings. According to that shocking survey (which included graphic details regarding the techniques of torture), Americans condoned barbaric crimes against Blacks because they believed that "Negro men are despoilers of the virtue of white women." Statistics, however, revealed that fewer than one-third of the victims had ever been charged with sexual assault; many, in fact, were accused of absolutely no offense at all. Wells' chilling conclusion: Lynching was "an excuse to get rid of Negroes who were acquiring wealth and property."

Predictably enough, *A Red Record* whipped more reactionary readers into a slavering white fury. According to the *New York Times*, the author was "a slanderous and nasty-minded mulattress;" another critic railed, "The black wretch who has written that foul lie should be tied to a stake at the corner of Main and Madison Street." Even a retired Black diplomat refuted her premise: "A reputable or respectable Negro has never been lynched and never will be," he proclaimed sanctimoniously.

But Wells would relinquish neither pen nor sword. "Not until the Negro rises in his might and takes a hand in resenting such cold-blooded murders, if he has to burn up whole towns, will a halt be called in wholesale lynchings," wrote the armed-and-dangerous activist; "A Winchester rifle should have a place of honor in every Black home."

> "I had already determined to sell my life as dearly as possible if attacked. I felt if I could take one lyncher with me, that would even up the score a little bit."
>
> —I. W.

Nellie Bly, née Elizabeth Cochrane Seaman (1865–1922)
In the Public Interest

The hallucinating harpy wasn't merely teetering on the verge of a nervous breakdown—she was plunging headlong into the abyss (weeping, writhing, babbling incoherently in Spanish). Blissfully ignorant of the madwoman's true identity, medics at New York's infamous Blackwell Island asylum simply yawned and added another hysterical female to the patient roster. Their mistake: Once again, Nellie Bly, undercover reporter for Joseph Pulitzer's popular

New York World, had gone over the deep end in pursuit of a story. And once again, the result would be a scathing exposé, this one disclosing no end of sordid details about the "human rat trap" at Blackwell Island.

Bly's brilliant career as a muckraker began in 1885 when she fired off an indignant response to an editorial in the *Pittsburgh Dispatch* entitled, "What Girls Are Good For" (not much, according to the author, apart from nursing and nurturing). Her letter persuaded the editor that this particular girl, at least, was good for writing assignments, and the eighteen-year-old wunderkind was soon covering sensationalistic stories about slums and sweatshops for the *Dispatch*.

It was as Pulitzer's protégée at the *World*, however, that Bly's talent for flamboyant editorial exhibitionism truly emerged. As an encore to her ersatz lunatic performance, she temporarily took up purse snatching and succeeded in obtaining an insider's view of prison life. (Just as she suspected, the conditions were squalid; and just as she anticipated, her published article was extraordinarily well received.) She went on to pose as a prostitute, extracting a shocking confession from a well-known pimp; another front-page headline, another round of kudos. And ever so briefly, she fluttered across the casting stage of a Broadway musical, fully confirming her theory that the chorus girl's life was no bed of roses. (The tights she was given did not fit, the celebrity reporter informed her fascinated following, while her standard-issue ballet slippers were too big.)

In 1889, Bly essayed her most ambitious role yet—that (as the *World* proudly proclaimed) of a "Feminine Phileas Fogg." Traveling by steamer, train, rickshaw, and burro, the one-woman media event managed to shave a good eight days off the globe-trotting record of the hero of Jules Verne's *Around the World in Eighty Days*. Naturally, she found much to fault along the way: abominable food, unattractive railway carriages—even the fog in Italy received a written reprimand. When she returned, she came as a conquering heroine; police had to clear a path for her triumphal march through the crowded streets of New York. Apparently now accustomed to moving at lightning speed, it didn't take Bly long to decide what to do with Robert Seaman, an elderly tycoon whom she married in 1895, just a week after their fortuitous introduction. "Few young women have had more worldly experience than Miss Bly," noted the *World*, "and few are more capable of enjoying the pleasures of a millionaire's existence." And few, it might also have been added, were more capable of ferreting out any flaws therein. But apparently none existed, for the scandalmongering reporter never filed one single story revealing the hidden horrors of life as a lady of leisure.

THE MEANDERING MUCKRAKER

"Complacency is a far more dangerous attitude than outrage."

—Naomi Littlebear

Harriet Beecher Stowe (1811–1896)
Perverse Prosaist

"I won't be any properer than I've a mind to be," declared novelist Harriet Beecher Stowe, and she wasn't. Uninvited and distinctly unwelcome, she often wandered into the garden of neighbor Mark Twain and snipped all the prettiest blooms. She took cocktails at eleven in the morning and claret in the afternoon, and she was once discovered in a drunken sprawl, her hoop skirt up around her head and her flowered garters on display. And just for the hell of it, Twain griped, she liked to sneak up behind some innocent victim or the other and let loose with "a war whoop that would jump that person out of his shoes."

According to husband Henry, Stowe wasn't any sweetheart at home, either; slothful and "slack," she tormented him by "wabbling" his newspapers "into one wabble and sprawling them on the table." "I must have a room to myself, which shall be my room," countered the housekeeper with higher ambitions, scooping Virginia Woolf by several decades. With six little Stowes scampering about, a writer's plea for privacy was understandable. But even when her offspring grew up and Stowe got her space, the maternal burden was too heavy to bear in silence: Writing letters to her children, she complained, sapped her creative energies.

When the misbehaving mother turned her attention to moral matters in 1852, however, America sat up and listened. A radical repudiation of the institution of slavery, *Uncle Tom's Cabin* (which sold three million copies before the Civil War) simultaneously provoked the wrath of Southern slaveholders and galvanized latent abolitionists into action. In the oft-repeated phrase of Abraham Lincoln, the author was "the little lady who wrote the book that made the big war." But chronically contrary Stowe wouldn't cop to the compliment. "I did not write it," she demurred; "God wrote it. I merely did his dictation."

As for *Lady Byron Vindicated*, Stowe's second successful stab at stirring up controversy, any supernatural assistance probably came from the opposite realm. First published by installment in 1869 in the *Atlantic Monthly*, the work thoroughly (and in several particulars, inaccurately) trashed the reputation of the revered Lord Byron, charging the deceased poet with incest and other acts too terrible for the Victorian imagination to contemplate. As a result, the *Atlantic* lost fifteen thousand subscribers, and the writer an even greater number of fans. But allegations that she had written a piece of pornography didn't faze scandal-mongering Stowe, who promptly proceeded to expand her erroneous exposé into a book. "Who cares what the critics say?" shrugged the occasionally popular yet eternally improper author.

THE PORN-PEDDLING HARRIET BEECHER STOWE

"I do not mean to live in vain."

—H. B. S.

Girl Meets Girl

Being well-bred ladies both, actress Annie Hindle and her dresser Annie Ryan knew just what to do when they discovered in 1886 that they had fallen in love. Not for this proud pair a shamefully furtive affair; the time-honored roommate ruse they apparently rejected out of hand. Nor did either retreat into a conventional marriage with a man just to keep up appearances. Instead, they declared their love to the world, and in a formal religious service in Grand Rapids, Michigan, took each other as lawfully wedded spouses before God, the Reverend Dr. E. H. Brooks, and Gilbert Saroney, a female impersonator who served as best man, as ballast no doubt for Annie Hindle, who was known for her work as a male impersonator. The ceremony completed, the new husband (resplendent in a dress suit) and the best man (resplendent in a dress) celebrated by sharing a bottle of wine and a cigarette as the blushing bride looked on demurely.

HOLY TERRORS AND POPE PERTURBERS

Mary Emerson (1774–1863)
Problematic Protestant

Fully prepared to meet her Maker at a moment's notice, Mary Emerson stalked the streets of Concord, Massachusetts decked out in a funeral shroud. As to the spiritual status of nephew Ralph Waldo Emerson, however, the curmudgeonly Christian had her doubts. The driving force in the early life of that revered religious rebel, Ms. Emerson deemed it her duty to see that young Ralph didn't commit the mortal sin of mediocrity.

"Scorn trifles," scolded the self-reliant spinster, who personally penned the prayers she forced her intelligent yet indolent relative to recite. Meekly, the future father of American transcendentalism turned his mind to higher matters. "She was as great an influence on my life as Greece or Rome," he would later remark of his austere aunt; "Her genius was the purest." As to the specific form such superlativity took, the ever-ethereal Mr. Emerson failed to specify. But all agreed that the troublemaking talents of the tiny tyrant (as Ms. Emerson stood just four foot, three inches) were considerably above average. "A person at war with society as to all its decorums, she eats and drinks what others do not, and when they do not," tattled one neighbor. Further, it was noted, she "enters into conversation with everybody, and talks on every subject." And even Emerson herself had to concede that she wasn't the cheeriest of chatterboxes. "To live to give pain rather than pleasure...seems the spider-like necessity of my being on earth," she sighed.

Indeed. Adapting the philosophy of Immanuel Kant into a more palatable American format, Ralph found, was child's play compared to satisfying his self-appointed mentor. "Would to God thou wouldst not to Cambridge," Ms. Emerson wrote when he was accepted at Harvard—an achievement customarily considered more cause for celebration than complaint. When the troubled transcendentalist left the church, Ms. Emerson spat that she would have preferred to shovel dirt on his grave than "to lose Waldo as I have lost him." Not until her now-notorious nephew's heretical address to the Harvard Divinity School in 1838, however, did Mary actually exercise the power of excommunication, withholding the dubious pleasure of her company and ceasing to speak to him altogether.

Under the circumstances, it is difficult to imagine that the resounding silence rendered Ralph's life significantly more unpleasant than before. As one candid obituarist noted on Mary Emerson's death in 1863, "She was thought to have the power of saying more disagreeable things in a half hour than any person living." But as the compulsive critic and her rebellious protégé proved in the end, those who dare to make waves inevitably leave a more lasting imprint on their era than those who merely make nice.

"Do what you are afraid to do."

—M. E.

The Clean-Minded Clergywoman

A lifetime subscriber to the theory that cleanliness is next to godliness, Sister Mary Catherine Cabreaux devoted precious little time to rosaries or raptures. Instead, the pragmatic postulant passed a seventeen-year stint in an Oregon City mission plucking lice from heathen heads, emptying evil-smelling latrines (other Sisters, she confessed, "could hardly remain near us in the Chapel"), and masterminding a bloodthirsty crusade against bedbugs. As to the latter, it seems, routing Beelzebub himself might have been a less arduous task. But with the Lord by her side (and perhaps more significant, a disinfectant fashioned from potassium and soap), "we succeeded in destroying millions of eggs," gloated God's most enthusiastic exterminator.

Elizabeth Cady Stanton (1815–1902)
The Goddess Within

When ever-so-egalitarian Elizabeth Cady Stanton said a prayer, she addressed it not only to the great patriarch in the sky, but to her "Heavenly Mother" as well. Not that Stanton—initiator of the historic Seneca Falls women's rights convention of 1848, first president of the National Woman's Suffrage Association, and author of numerous political pamphlets and books—spent much time on her knees. For one thing, she was far too busy trying to turn the world topsy-turvy. ("The usual masculine grace has long been a thorn in my flesh," she complained; "The rooster may do the crowing, but it is the faithful hen who lays the eggs.") Besides, Stanton found, the supplicant position simply didn't suit her.

"All the religions on the face of the earth degrade [us]," proclaimed the status-conscious suffragist; "So long as woman accepts the position that they assign her, her emancipation is impossible." As an antidote to the spiritual status quo, Stanton urged "spaniel wives" (as she termed her meeker sisters) to raise their voices in protest against the fallacy of male superiority. It was advisable, she noted pragmatically, to loosen the corset strings first, so as to render the lungs more powerful.

Just to set the historical record straight, Stanton also took it upon herself to analyze certain offensive Christian concepts in a feminist fashion the resulting tome—published in two volumes in 1895 and 1898—being titled *The Woman's Bible*. "In what way could children show their mothers honor?" read the characteristically arch commentary on the Fifth Commandment. "All the laws and customs forbid it." Politically correct as the new and improved Bible may have been, however, it found little favor even among Stanton's most radical peers. The burgeoning suffragist movement, they felt, could ill afford to lose the support of more God-fearing gender-mates.

If nothing else, however, Stanton's intense scrutiny of the scriptures did in the end allow her the small satisfaction of invoking biblical authority to her own advantage, just as men had done for centuries. During the course of a New York women's rights convention, a married clergyman, apparently one somewhat unclear on the fundamental concept of the conference, saw fit to scold Stanton for speaking in public. "The apostle Paul enjoined silence upon women," he chided; "Why don't you mind him?" "The apostle Paul," retorted the learned laywoman, "also enjoined celibacy upon the clergy. Why don't you mind him?"

STANTON PENNED *THE WOMAN'S BIBLE*

"The Bible and the Church have been the greatest stumbling blocks in the way of women's emancipation."

—E. C. S.

Ann Lohman (1812–1878)

Ladies' Choice

"Do not suffer your hand to be held or squeezed," advised *The Young Lady's Companion* in 1836, "without showing that it displeases you by instantly withdrawing it." Alas, withdrawal proved as ineffectual a barrier to conception in the Victorian era as in our own: by 1850, one abortion was performed for every five or six live births, and newspapers openly advertised the services of those skilled in treating "female complaints."

Notorious nationwide for catering to the needs of the prematurely pregnant was New York's Ann Lohman, who in 1836 hung out her shingle as "Madame Restell, female physician and professor of midwifery." At the time, her trade (which also included the dispensing of contraceptives) was not illegal in that state. But thanks to Lohman's aggressive advertising campaign, which aroused the wrath of both the American Female Reform Society and the Archbishop of New York, it was soon to become so. Arrested in 1847 for aborting a quickened fetus, Lohman stood trial on the charge of manslaughter and was sentenced to a term at Blackwell's Island prison. "Lust, licentiousness, seduction, and abortion, thundered the prosecutor, "would be the inevitable occurrences of every day" if the so-called "Wickedest Woman in the City" were allowed to pursue her profession.

During Lohman's twelve-month incarceration, however, rank carnality evidently flourished of its own accord; on her release, the women of New York clamored for her services even more loudly than before. By 1864, she was operating out of a fashionable four-story brownstone on Fifth Avenue—a site selected, rumor had it, expressly to annoy the archbishop, who was then erecting St. Patrick's Cathedral just two blocks away.

But even as Lohman prospered—at her death, her estate would be estimated at nearly a million dollars—neighborhood property values fell, and the lots flanking her miniature mansion stood vacant. The increasingly aristocratic abortionist, however, affected an indifferent attitude; she furnished her home in frankly opulent style, employed a full staff of servants, and was often seen riding in Central Park with a liveried footman. In short, shuddered the *New York Times*, she "ostentatiously flaunted her wealth and made an attractive part of the finest avenue in the city odious by her constant presence."

Lohman was not, however, to collect the wages of sin forever. In 1878, at the age of sixty-six, she was arrested by a vice officer on charges of selling articles intended for "immoral" use (otherwise known as birth control devices). But the conspicuous contraceptionist was never to have her day in court. On the morning of the trial (scheduled appropriately enough for April Fool's Day), Lohman was found dead in her bathtub, having slit her throat with a carving knife. In the words of the arresting officer, it was "a bloody ending to a bloody life." But to those weary of seeing women martyred in the never-ending war against sexual hypocrisy, it was simply a bloody shame.

"I have never injured anybody. Why should they bring this trouble upon me?"

—A. L.

Papal Bull

Perhaps the Vatican had something a little more Michelangelo in mind, but expatriate artist Anne Whitney refused to genuflect before the glory that was Rome. Perturbed by that city's indifference to its impoverished citizens, she sculpted an ancient beggar woman, and lest any should miss the point, titled the piece *Roma*. This begat such a brouhaha in the Papal Court of 1869 that

Maria Monk (1816–1849)

Not Any Nun

In the late twentieth century, the nation—or at least a select portion
of it—definitely had heard of adventuress-cum-author Sidney Biddle
Barrows. Scooping the "Mayflower Madam" by a century and a half,
however, was transplanted Canadian Maria Monk, who in 1836
translated her extremely colorful experiences as a fallen woman into a
lucrative library format. Titled *The Awful Disclosures of Maria Monk,
As Exhibited in a Narrative of Her Sufferings during a Residence
of Five Years as a Novice, and Two Years as a Black Nun, in the
Hôtel Dieu Nunnery at Montreal*, Ms. Monk's lengthy autobiography
purported to expose a "truth" both titillating and terrifying. No sooner
had the naïve novice taken her vows, she reported, than a lust-stricken
priest had dragged her off to "a private apartment" where he "treated
me in a brutal manner." Despite this inauspicious introduction to her
chosen career, however, Monk was to remain at the convent for a full
two years thereafter, too devoted to her vocation to be deterred by the
occasional group grope.

For far from a haven of holiness, she revealed, the Hôtel Dieu
resembled nothing so much as a veritable inferno of iniquity,
burgeoning with sadistic Fathers, all-too-acquiescent nuns, and their
resulting shameful progeny. Those innocent babes, incidentally, were
said to have been strangled at birth and casually deposited in the
cellar; sisters who said "no" suffered a similar fate. ("There were other
acts occasionally proposed and consented to, which I cannot name in a
book," added Monk, lest any reader fail to be sufficiently impressed by
the horrors heretofore detailed.) Fortunately, however, the writer was

not to remain a prisoner of priestly passions forever; impregnated by a clergyman, she engineered her escape and fled to New York, sparing her unborn child from the cemetery in the cellar.

Awful Disclosures enjoyed an immediate and phenomenal success, which was in no way diminished by the subsequent disclosure that the work was largely mendacious. As outraged investigators—Catholic and Protestant alike—soon learned, the twenty-year-old author had indeed borne a child to a priest. But the liaison in question had not occurred at the entirely innocuous Hôtel Dieu: Records revealed that Monk had been neither novice nor nun in that much-maligned convent, nor in any other. Indeed, the only Catholic institution in which she had ever passed much time was a mission for wayward women—a fact her own mother (who indicated that Monk had been prone to bizarre fantasies since childhood) was happy to verify.

Even in the case of incontrovertible evidence, however, book sales soared, and readers purchased more than 300,000 copies over the course of the next twenty-five years. Some attributed its success to sentiment against an increasing influx of Catholic immigrants, widely perceived as an economic threat by citizens of longer standing. But perhaps there was more to the story than that. Fraudulent as her tale may have been, Monk's triumph of the imagination underscored one universal truth: Sinners are always more interesting than saints, and hell-raisers infinitely more fascinating than angels.

"A lie told for the good of the church or Convent was meritorious, and of course the telling of it a duty."

—M. M.

SHAMELESS EXHIBITIONISTS AND NOTABLE NARCISSISTS

Isabella Stewart Gardner (1840–1924)
Beauty and the East

Famed for both her bosom and her Botticellis, scandalous socialite Isabella Gardner lived for beauty—particularly, it seems, her own. On the Boston Common, she strutted her shapely stuff in a frock so form-fitting that crowds gathered to stare. ("Saw Belle last night," wrote a friend; "Saw a *lot* of her!") Just for fun, she leashed a lion and paraded him up and down Boston's trendy Tremont Street, making quite a spectacle of her splendid self in the process. And for her famous 1887 portrait by painter John Sargent, she chose to pose in a *très décolleté* gown, one cut, as a particular gentleman gasped, "all the way down to Crawford's Notch."

Her anatomy, however, wasn't the only asset Gardner liked to flaunt. Courtesy of a Parisian finishing school, she possessed a taste for the finer things in life; thanks to a prosperous husband (and eventually, a two-million-dollar inheritance), she could also afford to collect the classic masterpieces she craved. But as well-bred Bostonians whispered behind her back, the acquisitive aesthete's tastes apparently didn't run to the Old Masters of Europe alone. At one swank soirée, guests got a good gander at boxer John L. Sullivan, who stripped to his trunks, and egged on by his hostess, flexed his perfect pectorals for all to admire. Young Henry James turned up from time to time, sighing in scores of mash notes to his beauteous Belle over "pretty little evenings" and "the harmony of your presence." For the lovesick Dr. Henry Bigelow, there seemed "to be no alternative but to sit...and think of the way your dress fits." And when Mr. James Whistler came to call, he made sure mama didn't tag along.

Apparently having worked out a satisfactory (if somewhat unusual) marital arrangement with his wife, Mr. Gardner obligingly turned a blind eye to the male harem in his home. But others were not so kind. Asked to contribute to the Boston Charitable Ear and Eye Association, the much-snubbed socialite snapped, "Really? I didn't know there *was* a charitable eye or ear in Boston." And when a snooty matron started to run on regarding her distinguished American Revolutionary ancestry, Gardner got in another dig at her detractors. "Ah yes," she muttered; "They were much less careful about immigration in those days, I believe."

In Gardner's case, however, beauty was eventually to conquer all. she would go down in history as neither libertine nor loudmouth, but rather as the woman who in 1903, made her city the great gift of the world-renowned Isabella Stewart Gardner Museum. But thought that glorious gallery overflowed with spoils plundered from the capitals of Europe—Titians, Rembrandts, and Raphaels among them—not every breathtaking *objet d'art* was an import. In the end, it seems, even Gardner was able to find some local loveliness that rivalled her own. As long as she lived, she insisted the museum was to be staffed exclusively by handsome Harvard men.

"I never expected gratitude."

—I. S. G.

Annie Taylor (1858–1921)

A Barrel of Fun

Described by one observer as a "plain, stout, old woman," Annie Taylor was scarcely the type of dazzling damsel whose very presence quickens the pulse and makes the heart sing. But for one brief moment on October 24, 1901, the forty-three-year-old schoolteacher was the most fascinating woman in America. Despite the fact that she didn't even know how to swim, the dumpy daredevil announced she was hell-bent on plummeting down Niagara Falls in a barrel.

As it turned out, that kamikaze plunge constituted one of the wackiest get-rich-quick schemes ever to ferment in an avaricious American mind. According to Taylor's line of reasoning, the Pan American Exposition then taking place in Buffalo was teeming with easy marks eager for a reason to throw their cash around. Purely by geographic coincidence, Niagara Falls was located just outside Buffalo. Seeing her opportunity, Taylor invested in a 160-pound oak barrel and hired a publicity agent.

Understandably, local officials weren't quite as thrilled by Taylor's proposed stunt as the thousands of rubberneckers who assembled to view it. To the coroner in particular, she looked like a lot of unwanted overtime just waiting to happen. But Taylor refused to back down; "If the authorities stop my attempt, I will jump to my death over the falls, and you will have to work for sure," she warned.

Shortly before four o'clock, the determined death defier (outfitted rather in rather funereal style in a long black gown) stepped into a small boat and was rowed by two male assistants to the launch point just above Horseshoe Falls. Discreetly, she waited until the spectators on shore had faded from view before slipping into a less cumbersome costume. "I think it would be unbecoming [in] a woman of my refinement and of my years to parade before a crowd in a short skirt," she explained delicately, allowing herself to be strapped into her barrel.

The dramatic descent through the raging waters took all of ten seconds: Taylor emerged from her vessel bruised and bleeding slightly behind one ear, but otherwise unharmed. "Nobody ought ever to do that again," she remarked insightfully, and spent the remainder of the afternoon giving interviews to an awestricken press.

Shortly thereafter, the momentary media sensation launched phase two of her self-promotion strategy—a lecture tour in which the "Queen of the Mist" planned to recount the historic events of October 24 for rapt audiences across the nation. But the honeymoon was already over, and Taylor—destined to perish in poverty some twenty years later—was no longer America's sensational new sweetheart. Ever fickle, the public quickly forgot all about that titillating ten-second thrill and stayed away in droves.

NO, THANK YOU

"I don't want to experience it again. I'd sooner be shot from a cannon."

—A. T.

Margaret Fuller (1810–1850)
Full of Herself

"I now know all the people worth knowing in America, and I find no intellect comparable to my own," brainy Bostonian Margaret Fuller once declared. And indeed, brought up on dinner-table debates with family friends Henry Thoreau, Ralph Waldo Emerson, and Bronson Alcott, the immodest ingenue blossomed into one of the most distinguished minds of her day. for better or worse, her ego evidently expanded accordingly. The author of the feminist classic *Woman in the Nineteenth Century* fancied herself, sniped one former friend, "the elect of the earth in intellect and refinement."

Then as now, however, smart women still suffered (perhaps even more acutely than their less scintillating sisters) from the sexist society blues, and Fuller deplored the "gentle miscommunication" of her gender from the life of the mind. To compensate, high-IQ heretics were encouraged to share their analyses of Goethe or Greek mythology at the weekly "Conversations" she hosted during the late 1830s. (Not surprisingly, the participants also held forth at length on the future of feminism in America.) As to the inevitable comparison with France's formidable Madame de Staël, Fuller insisted she herself was the superior *salonière*: "While [de Staël] was instructing you as a mind," Fuller explained, "she wished to be admired as a Woman." Not so Boston's headstrong hostess (self-described as "bright and ugly"), who wished only to be—and frequently was—admired as a Genius.

Still, there was more than passing merit to Fuller's boast that she was "chosen among women." Acclaimed for her work as a literary critic at the *New York Tribune*, she also served in the 1840s as editor of *The Dial*, New England's most prestigious philosophical journal. Oddly enough, however, the brilliant wordsmith was apparently unable to distinguish between the roles of editor and writer-in-chief; her own contributions frequently comprised more than half the contents of the publication. (*"The Dial,"* as one historian wryly noted, "so often thought of as the journal of American 'transcendentalism,' was, during her editorship, the journal of Margaret Fuller.")

Lest her supreme solipsism not raise enough eyebrows, Fuller went on to flaunt a two-year affair with radical Italian revolutionary Giovanni d'Ossoli, formalizing the union only when compelled to do so by pregnancy. But if Boston took a predictably dim view of the liaison, the great thinker refused to bother her capacious cranium with such pettiness. "I accept the universe," she proclaimed magnanimously. ("By God, she'd better!" retorted Thomas Carlyle, the eminent Scottish historian.) But such largesse was lost on the indifferent cosmos; in 1850, forty-year-old Fuller perished in a dramatic shipwreck on the high seas. One suspects, however, that she would not have been entirely surprised—nor, in fact, entirely dismayed—by that tragic twist of fate. "For precocity," the self-acknowledged savant once observed, "some great price is always demanded sooner or later in life."

"The soft arms of affection will not suffice for me, unless on them I see the steel bracelets of strength."

—M. F.

Elisabet Ney (1833–1907)
Monumental Egotist

Every inch the eccentric artist, Elisabet Ney experienced quite an epiphany when she purchased a particularly dilapidated piece of Texas property in 1873. "Here will I live! And here will I die!" the German-born sculptor predicted dramatically, if not entirely accurately. Few of the brazen bohemian's new neighbors, however, were delighted by the prospect of her lengthy tenure in that liberal-loathing territory. Nor did it occur to them that Ney, widely renowned in Europe for her bust of Bismarck, might be considered an important personage by anyone other than herself. Unacquainted with the genre of the rebellious genius, the provincial population saw only a risqué redhead who flouted—with apparent glee—every prevailing standard of propriety.

Reluctant to concede she had ever been a bourgeois bride, Miss Ney (as she insisted on calling herself) found it more palatable to pass off her Scottish spouse as "my best friend" and her perfectly legitimate son as a bastard. Her wardrobe (which ran to Grecian togas, or alternately, white trousers and black frock coats) was frankly designed to shock, and it succeeded admirably in that goal. Indeed, the local chapter of the Ku Klux Klan—an organization whose own peculiar sartorial standard was the bedsheet—once considered the contents of Miss Ney's closet and decreed (rather ineffectually, as it turned out) that she should stick to skirts.

Even when it came to cultivating potential patrons, Ney would not bow to convention. Rejecting outright the role of hostess, she rebuffed callers with the admonition that she would send for them if and when she was so inclined. To the few who dared offer the hospitality of their own homes, she presented a list of nonnegotiable demands. "I must be provided with a hammock to sleep in," the assertive artist informed wealthy Sarah Pease, Austin's reigning socialite. And, she added, meat must not appear on the menu: "Even to sit at a table where human beings are devouring the flesh of dead animals is for me most nauseating." Fortunately, Mrs. Pease (who would join Paderewski, Pavlova, and Caruso in Ney's circle of intimate friends) shared her guest's conviction that genius need not cater to common convention. Obligingly, she cleared her table of corpses and even spotted the sculptor a loan.

Posthumously touted as "the founder of art in Texas," Ney received extravagant national acclaim at Chicago's Columbian Exposition in 1893 for her outsized statues of Sam Houston and Stephen Austin—

and, at last, the wholehearted approbation of her adopted state. Never one to kowtow to Texan tastes, however, the artist herself considered a depiction of the murderous Lady Macbeth her crowning achievement. Indeed, she confessed, the work was so brilliant that she was herself unable to gaze upon it for more than a few minutes at a time, lest she be completely overwhelmed by its beauty.

"I am truly void of what one would call patriotism."

—E. N.

The Naked Truth

Contrary to popular belief, the Wild West of the late nineteenth century was actually quite a civilized place. In fact, a young lady could safely stroll the streets in garmentless glory, should she so choose...or so claimed "Prairie Rose," a toothsome tart who on a dare sauntered down Main Street of a Kansas cow town *au naturel* and lived to tell the tale. Of course, would-be molesters were probably a tad intimidated by the loaded pistol she carried in each hand.

SCANDALOUS SOCIALITES AND HELL-RAISING HEIRESSES

Jane Addams (1860–1935)
Seasoned Slummer

Poor Jane Addams. The head of her class at Rockford Female Seminary in 1881, she suffered through the remainder of the decade with a bad case of the post-graduation blues. The *de rigueur* European tour failed to amuse. The prospect of tying the knot with Mr. George Haldeman, the suitor of her stepmother's choice, plunged her into "the nadir of...nervous depression." And somehow, it seemed, there ought to be more to life than pouring tea and planning Chicago charity balls. "I was absolutely at sea as far as any moral purpose was concerned," she admitted in her autobiography.

So what was a disaffected debutante to do? "I gradually became convinced that it would be a good thing to rent a house," she concluded. An adorable little bachelor girl flat, however, wasn't quite what Addams had in mind. For the socialite who suddenly sprang a social conscience, only an address on the wrong side of the tracks would do—in "a part of the city where many primitive and actual needs are found." And as roommates, she frankly sought other female malcontents: persons who found a life of privilege problematic and jaded academics who yearned to "learn of life from life itself." Far from a disaster, however, Addams' new domicile was destined to become the successful social experiment known as Hull House—a haven for the impoverished immigrants of Chicago's Nineteenth Ward and a heaven-sent opportunity for scores of wealthy ennui victims to do something worthwhile with their lives.

Thus, in the early 1890s, the former star of Rockford could be seen rolling up her silken sleeves to midwife the birth of an illegitimate baby. She appeared on the filth-strewn streets at dawn to dog a callous garbage collector, insisting that he carry away even the lowly slum-dwellers' trash. Into sweltering sweatshops and crowded tenements she sauntered, and she dared to publish her findings in *Hull-House Maps and Papers*, a landmark study of nineteenth-century urban squalor.

But if Addams' once-manicured fingernails now bore traces of the workingman's dirt, her breeding nonetheless betrayed itself at every turn. When a famous chain-smoking reformist paid a call, the diplomatic hostess puffed the only cigarette of her life to put her guest at ease. She paved the way for travels with close companion Mary Rozet Smith by wiring ahead for a double bed, tactfully avoiding any unseemly on-site discussions of sleeping arrangements. And to the end of her life, she was plagued by otherworldly messages from her now-deceased stepmother, who scolded her soundly for rejecting a more conventional mode of existence.

Regardless of family feelings concerning the matter, however, Hull House was to become the national model for social reform in the industrial age. Though unique in 1891, by 1910, four hundred similar settlements had sprung up across the country. Further, by drawing attention to the plight of the hitherto invisible immigrant, Addams helped open the door for humanitarian modifications to child labor laws, working conditions for women, and industrial safety standards. And, one can only assume, such altruistic accomplishments also helped assuage any lingering pangs of liberal guilt suffered by the college graduate who chose to live in the ghetto.

> "I had at last finished with the everlasting 'preparation for life,' however ill-prepared I might be."
>
> —J. A.

Self-Made Millionaire

Con artist "Goldbrick" Cassie Chadwick saw no reason why a woman shouldn't make her own money. In the late 1890s, the Canadian career criminal manufactured five million dollars' worth of promissory notes from capitalist Andrew J. Carnegie, who would no doubt have been surprised to learn he was supposed to be her papa. When the scam was finally discovered, it was clear that Chadwick wasn't good for the sizeable sums she'd drawn on the imaginary IOUs. She also wasn't good for the Citizens National Bank of Oberlin, Ohio, which collapsed due to her fraudulent fantasies.

HER DEAR NOT-PAPA

Harriet Hubbard Ayer (1849–1903)
About Face

In 1886, Chicago's more elite citizens were not entirely displeased when socialite Harriet Ayer committed the *faux pas* of divorcing her wealthy-yet-wandering husband. All along, they had suspected that there was something not quite nice about a society hostess who served sauterne with Sunday breakfast, counted the flaming, flamboyant Oscar Wilde among her admirers, and displayed far too great an interest (and, it seemed, an excessive amount of herself) in avantgarde Parisian fashions. And when the former lady of leisure took out a $50,000 loan and started manufacturing and selling beauty cream to support herself, her critics' darkest fears were delightfully confirmed. Ladies, as everyone knew, didn't dip into the rouge pot or anything remotely resembling it; needless to say, they also refrained from trafficking in tawdry commerce.

Acquainted from birth with the psychology of the privileged, however, Ayer knew precisely how to put the best possible face on her bold new enterprise. The controversial product, she claimed, was scarcely designed for floozies; indeed, her exotic recipe had once been the private property of Madame Recamier, a great beauty of Napoleon's day. As another sop to snob appeal, the creative cosmetician managed to secure the earnest testimonials of numerous famous belles—among them Sarah Bernhardt, Lillian Russell, and the Princess of Wales. According to actress Lily Langtry, in fact, Recamier creams were fully capable of removing "tan, sunburn, and the many annoying blemishes women, especially in the changeable climate of this country, are subjected to." (If nothing else, this rather alarming endorsement proved that Ayer's promotional tactics were quite advanced for her era: Langtry was at the time living free of charge in her home.)

By 1896, when Ayer began publishing a weekly beauty column in the *New York World*, tastefully painted ladies were appearing on the nation's finest boulevards—and not coincidentally, in factories and offices from coast to coast—with perfect impunity. Unquestionably, the former socialite's face-saving strategies had done much to pave the way for the widespread acceptance of artifice. In Ayer's opinion, however, the increasingly polished appearance of the American woman was no superficial matter. According to her, as females entered the work force in greater numbers, they discovered that donning war paint was *de rigueur* in competing for jobs. "Not all of them liked it, but they were quick to find out that youth and good looks gave them an advantage over plainer rivals," she wrote. Still, as the self-made cosmetics tycoon would have been the first to conceded, makeup did not constitute the exclusive foundation for feminine accomplishment. For women who wanted to succeed in a rapidly expanding world, it was, naturally, necessary to do far more with their heads than merely decorate them.

"I have very expensive tastes."

—H. H. A.

Henrietta Green (1834–1916)
Miserly Millionaire

Having learned all about the bulls and the bears at her well-to-do daddy's knee, financier Henrietta Green astonished everyone except herself by parlaying a ten-million-dollar inheritance into ten times that amount during the late nineteenth century. "There is no great secret in fortune making," shrugged the woman known in financial circles as the "Witch of Wall Street;" "All you have to do is buy cheap and sell dear, act with thrift and shrewdness, and be persistent." Of course, it also didn't hurt to have Green's uncanny instinct for converting her assets to cash just before a panic, or her competence at calculating the interest to be extracted from less prescient souls.

But if the richest woman in the world took her golden thumb for granted, perpetuating her prosperity constituted a never-ending source of angst. "Never...give anyone anything, not even a kindness," Green's protective papa had told her. True to her training, she boarded in tawdry hotels, subsisted on rice and other odd scraps, and never, ever, tipped a waiter. Nor, to her mind, could she afford to look like even a fraction of a million bucks. "They say I am cranky or insane because I dress plainly and do not spend a fortune on my gowns," shrugged the nation's worst-dressed moneylender. "Plainly," however, was putting it politely: Her garments actually grew green with age before she discarded them, and by her own admission, she saved a significant sum by laundering only the bottom layer of her petticoats. Evidently Green economized on soap as well, for her fingers were often black as a banker's heart from their compulsive perambulations through her plump portfolios of stocks and bonds.

Even in the bosom of her family, it seems, the unfashionable usurer found it necessary to maintain a vigilant guard against greed. Husband Edward signed a prenuptial waiver of any claim to her fortune, but he was nonetheless banished from her bed when he went bankrupt in 1885. ("My husband is of no use to me," she was subsequently heard to complain; "I wish I did not have him.") Son Ned hobbled through life with only one leg due to Mama's miserly ways: Green refused to pay for medical care after an unfortunate sledding accident, with the eventual result that the limb had to be amputated. Only her dog Dewey, in fact, saw the softer side of the coldhearted capitalist. "He loves me," she explained, "and he doesn't know how rich I am."

On occasion, however, the frugal financier could be coaxed to part with a modicum of advice. "Never speculate on Wall Street," she told peg-legged Ned in a moment of rare generosity. (Also, she added, he should "stay out of draughts.") But for the presumptuous freeloader who asked her to suggest a good investment, Green had precious few words to spare: "The other world," snapped the paranoid profiteer.

"I am in earnest; therefore they picture me as heartless."

—H. G.

Cash Cows

In 1885, Henrietta King survived the death of her spouse only to inherit the Texas-sized debts on his sprawling southwestern spread. Rising to the challenge, the novice rancher pared the enterprise of excess fat, developed some tasty new types of cattle, and pioneered a passel of novel techniques in meat production. When hardworking Henrietta died in 1925 at the age of ninety-two, the assets of her world-renowned ranch totaled over five million dollars, and the well-heeled widow had no further beef with her husband.

Molly Brown (1867–1932)
The Golden Rube

Having landed herself in Leadville, Colorado, specifically to seek her fortune, seventeen-year-old Molly Tobin (soon to be Brown) was initially unswayed by the passionate proposals of a local mining foreman. Her heart, she told him in no uncertain terms, lusted only for lucre. But gentlemanly Jim pressed his suit politely, and in 1886, he finally got his girl. And owing to his subsequent $2.5 million strike, his avaricious missus finally got her gold.

It quickly became apparent, however, that the new millionaires didn't have the foggiest notion of how to handle money. The story circulated that she once secreted away $300,000 in the cookstove, only to have the cache go up in flames around dinnertime. In fact, it would later turn out, the amount in question was only seventy-five dollars; and as it consisted solely of gold coinage, neither money nor marriage suffered significant damage in the blaze. ("Oh, hell," Brown cackled; "What difference does it make? It's a damn good story!")

Soon, however, Brown was burning through the family fortune with greater success. Having installed her spouse and herself in an expansive Denver manse, she sashayed through the city streets wrapped in so many layers of sable that one unkind soul dubbed her "a unique fur-bearing animal." But even $2.5 million couldn't purchase an entrée into Denver society, which simply snickered behind Brown's nouveau riche back. (Her voice, it was said, was like a train whistle; her gaudy gowns resembled Christmas trees.) Once, she managed to snag an invitation to call on exclusive society hostess Mrs. Horace Bennett. But the visit was not a success, as Brown's concept of interesting conversation consisted largely of inquiring as to the cost of Mrs. Bennett's pricey furnishings, and whistling in amazement at the responses.

Years later, when certain historic events transformed Brown from a strikingly untalented social climber into the "unsinkable" heroine of the *Titanic*, her poor social skills would constitute somewhat less cause for concern. "Row, you sons of bitches!" she reportedly bellowed to the two dozen fainthearted ladies she bullied into boarding a lifeboat; "Row, or I'll let daylight into you!" Meekly, the women picked up the oars and paddled away from disaster; few of *them* ever faulted Brown for her rough language or criticized her lack of decorum.

But that was in 1912, in the remote reaches of the North Atlantic Ocean. In mainstream nineteenth-century America, however, even a very wealthy woman couldn't afford to make a spectacle of herself. Sad to say, even once-smitten Jim grew increasingly less tolerant of his spouse's conspicuous antics. The final straw snapped when he returned home one evening to discover a convention of Cheyenne tribesmen in progress on his front lawn, their tepees pitched in the grass. The rubberneckers driving by to gape at Mrs. Brown's guests thought it was a hoot. Jim, however, was distinctly unamused, and he walked out then and there, never to return. To his credit, however, he did continue to support his gauche, guileless gold-digger in the style to which she never quite became accustomed.

"Sure, I'm eccentric. But I have a heart as big as a ham!"

—M. B.

Mary Ellen Pleasant, a.k.a. Mammy Pleasant (1814–1904)
The Root of All Evil

"Mammy Pleasant: Angel or Arch Fiend in the House of Mystery?" So ran the lurid headline in one San Francisco newspaper in 1899. In a sense, that rather slanderous sobriquet might be considered a compliment: Few females, after all—let alone those who were former slaves—were thought to warrant front-page billing in that era. On a significantly less sanguine note, however, San Francisco never could resolve its ambivalent feelings about the wealthy Black woman who influenced the city's economic and political course for over fifty years.

Pleasant arrived in California in 1850 with a price on her head, thanks to her work with the Underground Railroad, and several thousand dollars in her pocket, courtesy of a recently deceased spouse. Under the circumstances, she could afford to laugh at a local tycoon's offer to pay her five hundred dollars a month as a domestic. Instead, she invested in her own boardinghouse and saw to it that the ambience— far more elegant than that of similar San Francisco establishments—

appealed to top-drawer businessmen and politicians. Just as planned, this shrewd self-introduction to the city's financial aristocracy paid off handsomely. Having parlayed her nest egg into a small fortune, the ambitious entrepreneur went on to invest in real estate, lend short-term notes at usurious rates, and ultimately, even advise her monetary mentors on their own financial affairs. "She handled more money during pioneer days in California," wrote one historian, "than any other colored person."

Legend has it that Pleasant contributed $30,000 to fund John Brown's raid on Harpers Ferry in 1859. More verifiably—and certainly more successfully—she struck her own personal blow for civil rights in 1864, suing two San Francisco streetcar companies for refusing her the right to board. But Pleasant was not to escape punishment for her worldly savoir faire: Throughout her years in San Francisco, she would be plagued by an unsavory reputation as a voodoo artist. indeed, one sensational divorce trial in 1881 centered around the question of whether the savvy financier (labeled a "scheming, trafficking, crafty old woman" by the judge) had sold occult love potions to the wife.

Not until 1892, however, when millionaire Thomas Bell fell to his death in Pleasant's ornate thirty-room house (the so-called House of Mystery) did the city begin to scrutinize the alleged sorceress with a truly evil eye. According to the coroner, the death was entirely accidental, but many imaginative citizens found it more interesting to believe that Pleasant was personally responsible for the demise of her long-term business associate. Some said that Bell had refused to invest a large sum as she suggested, so she shoved him down the staircase. More popular (and infinitely more titillating) was the theory that Pleasant had simply voodooed him to death. Even in unconventional San Francisco, it was incomprehensible that a Black woman could succeed in a white man's world solely on the basis of her own intelligence and sophistication. The only logical explanation, obviously, was Black magic.

> "I run the show, and I'm a whole theater in myself."
>
> —M. E. P.

Miriam Leslie (1836–1914)
Imperishable Publisher

Like most esoteric modes of existence, the literary life isn't quite as glamorous as those who live it like to imply. But by the age of forty-four, New York magazine editor Miriam Leslie had indeed been everywhere and done everything and—judging by her lengthy list of amorous liaisons—almost everyone. In 1867, she waltzed with Bismarck at a swank soiree in the Tuileries. A decade later, she breezed through the brothels and opium dens of San Francisco, then stopped in Salt Lake City to conduct an innuendo-laden interview with the polygamous prophet Brigham Young. She hobnobbed with Cornelius Vanderbilt and Brazilian Emperor Don Pedro II and showed up at one exclusive reception wearing, it was noted, "$70,000 worth of diamonds upon her person." And in between (or on occasion, during) flirtations, she managed to fit in four assorted husbands, including Charles Kingsbury Wilde, the wan, weak-willed brother of infamous Oscar.

One thing which even the worldly-wise Ms. Leslie had never done, however, was to preside over a vast editorial empire. But in 1880, the death of her third spouse, magazine magnate Frank Leslie, catapulted the journalistic jetsetter into one of the most prestigious publishing positions in the nation. Unfortunately, as she soon discovered, her literary legacy also included several bankrupt publications and seventeen pending lawsuits. But to an accomplished coquette like Ms. Leslie, wooing back a straying readership looked like the most interesting challenge of her life. During the following five years, the suddenly serious socialite guided the company through a successful overhaul, pruning the poor performers among its periodicals and concentrating instead on *Frank Leslie's Popular Monthly*. Modestly advertised as "the cheapest and best Magazine in the world," the *Monthly* was perhaps also the only magazine whose editor preferred to hire women as writers and men as office help. Under the aegis of "the Empress of Journalism," the firm flourished; combined circulation jumped from 30,000 to an unprecedented 250,000, and Leslie's annual salary expanded accordingly, reaching $100,000 by 1885.

No longer the life of the press party, the born-again businesswoman now rose at dawn to pump iron and breakfast on beefsteak. "I have seen her...as cruel as the iceberg," said protégée Ella Wilcox; the poet Joaquin Miller compared her to Napoleon. But to Leslie—who by now had legally changed her first name to Frank—complaints about her lack of femininity were of little consequence. Boasted the former glamour girl, who was to leave a million dollars in her will "for the furtherance of the cause of Woman's Suffrage": "There is, I suppose, no girl in the world so perfectly capable of taking care of herself and doing it as well as the American girl."

"Make your mark and achieve success, or if need be, die in the attempt."

—M. L.

EDITREX EXTRAORDINAIRE

SOUTHERN REBELS AND CAPITAL OFFENDERS

Mary Boykin Chestnut (1823–1886)
Uncivil Warrior

War is hell. But it seems that Mary Boykin Chestnut, whose 400,000-word *Diary from Dixie* constitutes the most comprehensive (not to mention most verbose) surviving chronicle of the Civil War years, was fully prepared to send her spouse straight to the devil. So far as the South Carolina secessionist was concerned, the big guns of the Confederacy (including husband John, the first US senator to resign in protest following Lincoln's election in 1860) were proceeding about as speedily as a funeral procession. "Oh, if I could put some of my reckless spirit into these discreet, cautious, lazy men!" she wrote.

As the *Diary* made abundantly (though perhaps inadvertently) clear, Chestnut's desire to deposit John squarely in harm's way wasn't strictly a matter of politics. Having apparently graduated magna cum laude from the Strong & Silent school of masculine behavior, her husband "could see me...hung, drawn, and quartered without moving a muscle," complained the cantankerous chatterbox. Nor did he ever quite comprehend why Chestnut—like many erstwhile Southern belles, a dyed-in-the-wool party animal—couldn't curb her rambunctious social life, let alone curtail periodic private opium binges. And on the topic of his relationship with a certain "very haughty and highly painted dame," he had absolutely nothing to say—other, of course, than to deny everything. ("What a credulous fool you must take me to be," harped his helpmeet.)

John's militant Mrs., however, was completely capable of giving as good (or bad) as she got: When the ex-governor of South Carolina cast a lascivious look in her direction, she boldly returned his smoldering gaze. "I can make any body love me if I choose," she boasted, and indeed, the passionate politico was soon her constant companion. Suffice it to say that this defensive offense had the desired effect. After a full week of fuming while his wife entertained "the handsomest man on earth" under his own roof, laconic John finally let loose with a torrent of jealous invective. "Is it not too funny," chortled a greatly gratified Chestnut; "He is so *prosy.*"

Oddly enough, however, the warmongering wife was devastated when she realized in 1861 that John would soon see active duty. "I feel he is my all and I should go mad without him," she confessed to her *Diary.* That entry, however, was eventually erased; later readers could just make out the smudged lettering on the page, telltale evidence of the bedrock of love beneath the blazing matrimonial battlefield. On the domestic front as on the national, it seems, no warrior who hoped to survive could afford to wax sentimental, nor to acknowledge her deep underlying kinship with the enemy.

"There is no slave, after all, like a wife."

—M. C.

Not Dancing with Herself

In her salad days, Peggy Eaton, rumored to have performed the horizontal hootchy-kootchy quite prenuptially with her politically prominent husband, was known as Washington's most outrageous spouse. In fact, her wandering ways were even the official topic of a cabinet meeting in 1830. Nearly thirty years later, Eaton—now a badly behaved widow—set tongues wagging anew when she eloped with her own granddaughter's dancing teacher. Not until she had boned

Rose Greenhow (1815–1864)
The Talkative Traitor

Like every socialite worth her salted peanuts, Washington widow Rose Greenhow (touted by the *New York Herald* as "a bright and shining light" in the *haute culture* world of the capital) urged her guests to gossip. In contrast to DC's fluffier femmes, however, Ms. Greenhow didn't have to feign fascination when cocktail chatter turned to military matters. A secret secessionist sympathizer, her aim was to extract every ounce of relevant information from her well-placed Union connections.

Thanks to Greenhow's talented ears, the Battle of Bull Run in July, 1861—pegged by the Union as an easy victory—resulted in a resounding Confederate triumph. "I was almost as well advised of the strength of the hostile army in my front as is commander," gloated Gen. Pierre Beauregard of the Confederate Army. For her role in the victory, Greenhow received the compliments of Jefferson Davis ("But for you," he acknowledged, "there would have been no battle of Bull Run") and $2,500.

Greenhow was, of course, neither the first nor the last Washington woman to support the South. "Although I was never in the least danger of being diverted from my purpose," wrote one Union officer, "yet I well remember how often I was lured to the brink of the precipice." But federal authorities had always looked the other way; handcuffing one's hostess, after all, simply wasn't the done thing.

When the humiliating Bull Run syndrome persisted, however, Union General George McClellan scrapped the chivalric code of honor. "She knows my plans better than Lincoln or the Cabinet," he complained, "and has four times compelled me to change them." In August 1861, the legendary detective Allen Pinkerton arrested Greenhow on her doorstep, where she gallantly attempted to swallow a coded message. Even from her cell in the Old Capital Prison, however, she continued to annoy McClellan by waving a Confederate flag from her window and claiming that no one could capture her soul.

Released after two years on the condition that she vanish from Union territory, Greenhow complied by running the blockade and sailing to Europe. There she continued to rail away about rebellion, scoring some significant booty from sympathetic aristocrats. But South was never to see one sou of the earnings of that far-flung fundraising campaign. As Greenhow headed home in October 1864, her ship was spotted by Union patrols off the coast of Delaware and she was forced to flee in a tiny rowboat. For years a martyr-in-the-making, the chatty Confederate was finally silenced by the unforgiving sea, preceding the rather less splashy demise of her doomed raison d'être by only a few months.

> "I am a Southern woman, born with
> revolutionary blood in my veins."
>
> —R. G.

She Worked in Ladies' Wear

Unlike other Mata Haris of the Civil War era, Confederate spy Nancy Hart wasn't any cross-dresser. But that label certainly ended up applying to the unfortunate Union man who held her hostage in 1861, threatening from time to time to let his troops have their way with her. Though Hart managed to escape unscathed, she never forgot her tormentor's face. The next time she met up with the miserable oaf, she forced him to don one of her gowns, tethered him to her horse, and paraded the corseted captive around town for hours.

Mary Todd Lincoln (1818–1882)
A National Disgrace

In the late twentieth century, budget-conscious citizens would have their fun at the expense of First Ladies Jackie and Nancy—and, it seems, vice versa. But the curse of compulsive shopping didn't afflict latter-day leading ladies alone. Mary Lincoln appeared to suffer from the malady—though she preferred to pass it off as patriotism. "I must dress in costly material," decreed the spendthrift White House spouse, from 1861 to 1863 the nation's most conspicuous consumer; "The people scrutinize every article that I wear with critical curiosity."

And indeed, so the people did—though not in quite the manner Mary intended. "The weak-minded Mrs. Lincoln," one Oregon senator had occasion to note, "had her bosom on exhibition, and a flowerpot on her head." The president, casting a dubious gaze on her massive hoops, chimed in with his two cents worth: "Mother, if some of that tail were nearer the head, it would be in better style." Nonetheless, Mother Lincoln thought it unconscionable to economize on her controversial couture; duties on imported goods, she reasoned, swelled the nation's coffers, therefore she had a duty to spend.

No one hoped more fervently than Mrs. Lincoln, toward the end of her husband's first term in 1864, that he would remain in office for a second. During her four-year reign of error, the president's wife had seldom failed to avail herself of generous credit offers at the toniest East Coast emporia. Now nearly $30,000 in debt, she grew frantic. "If he is reelected, I can keep him in ignorance of my affairs," she wailed, "but if he is defeated, then the bills will be sent in, and he will know all." One novel solution came to mind: "The Republican politicians must pay my debts." Not surprisingly, however, few gentlemen so petitioned fully comprehended their duty to set the First Lady square with Lord & Taylor. Fortunately, the voters extricated Mary from her predicament before she could execute her backup plan of hawking manure from the White House lawn.

But a final reckoning was not far in the future. Lincoln was assassinated, of course, just three months into his second term, and the overextended widow was obliged to swear off her shopping sprees. Naturally, the "vampyre press" (as Mary termed the media) had a field day when it discovered the former first lady had consigned the bulk of her infamous wardrobe to a resale store in New York. "If I had committed murder in every state in this blessed Union, I could not be more traduced," sighed the desperate debtor, who never did quite catch on to the concept of checks and balances. "An ungrateful country, this."

THE SIXTEENTH FIRST LADY

"All that I ever did was actuated by the purest motives."
—M. T. L.

Maybelle Mitchell (1872–1918)
Too Tough for Tara

Maybelle Mitchell would have taken a torch to Tara, had she suspected for one second that Scarlett O'Hara was fashioned in her form. Though *Gone with the Wind* was penned by Mitchell's own daughter, the fiercest feminist in turn-of-the-century Atlanta would never have approved of that wasp-waisted, waffle-headed sex kitten whose main aim in life was matrimony. But evidently Miss Margaret knew Mom better than that. It was not shallow Scarlett, after all, but bold Rhett Butler—the swashbuckling trend-bucker who never did quite succeed in raising his sweetheart's consciousness—whom she modeled after Mama.

Frankly, Mother Mitchell (founder of the Atlanta Women's Study Club and a scorcher of a suffragist) didn't give a damn for women who spent their lives wandering aimlessly among the wisteria. And according to her daughter, "nothing infuriated her so much as the complacent attitude of other ladies who felt that they should let the gentlemen do the voting." Nor was Mrs. Mitchell just whistling Dixie on the great and glorious day when Carrie Chapman Catt roared into town—she toted her tiny tot (a Votes-for-Women banner tied around her tummy) right along to the rally. Not only that, but after hissing "blood-curdling threats" about what would happen if missy didn't mind her manners, she deposited her "between the silver pitcher and the water glasses while she made an impassioned speech."

But apparently the propaganda didn't penetrate, for soon six-year-old Margaret could be heard proclaiming that school was a supreme waste of time. it was her sole ambition, announced the aspiring young airhead, "to just grow up and marry a wealthy gentleman." But Mama would hear no such fiddle-dee-dee from the girl whom she dreamed would be a great feminist of the future. In a fit of progressive pique, she hitched up the buggy, plopped her disgraced daughter on the seat, and headed for the decaying-mansion district of Atlanta. There amidst the symbolic rubble, recalled Margaret, "She told me that my own world was going to explode under me someday, and God help me if I didn't have some weapon to meet the new world."

Adamant that her little lady learn to "do as boys do," Mitchell would in the future teach her to pull a trigger without trembling. (In the same tough-love vein, she was also known to slap her with a slipper for the heinous crime of shyness.) But Mama wasn't rapping about rifles that day in the ruins. "For God's sake," she snapped, "go to school and learn something that will stay with you. The strength of women's hands isn't worth anything, but what they've got in their heads will carry them as far as they need to go." And as far as she was concerned, obviously, Tara was far from the end of the road.

> "Scarlett thought in despair: 'Nothing, no nothing, she taught me is of any help to me!' 'Oh, Mother, you were wrong!' "
>
> —Gone with the Wind

Organized Criminal

Had the prudish Montana prosecutor been able to utter the word "brothel," he might have been able to make the charges stick. But according to the 1861 testimony of alleged madam "Chicago Joe," it was simply absurd to assert that she operated a "hurdy-gurdy house." True, Joe informed the court, she was guilty of possessing a piano; on occasion, her guests had even disported themselves to the shameless strains of violin music. But no déclassé barrel organ, she insisted, had ever darkened her door. Unable to produce the specific instrument in question, the prosecution was forced to concede defeat, and the semantically astute defendant waltzed away scot-free.

TOTALLY TRANSCENDENT TRAVELERS

Frances Willard (1839–1898)
Biker Chic

The cycling craze of the 1890s rolled across the nation like an 8.5 earthquake, with freewheeling females flying through the streets and disapproving doomsayers collapsing beneath heaps of rhetorical rubble. Not only did the sweaty new breed of scofflaws run the risk of developing pigeon toes and "bicycle eye," it was suggested, but the "unfettered liberty" of bicycling tended to "intoxicate" them to unspecified—though no doubt shocking—acts of immorality. Weighing in on the side of the exercise enthusiasts in 1895 was Women's Christian Temperance Union president Frances Willard, who emphatically did not endorse either intoxication or immorality. She did, however, urge women to take up the two-wheeler, singing its praises in *How I Learned to Ride the Bicycle*, her personal paean to the pedal. Contrary to popular opinion, Willard soberly stated, there were "high moral uses in the bicycle" and she would wholeheartedly "commend it as a teacher without pulpit or creed."

As the newly fit fifty-three-year-old was the first to concede, she had occasionally tumbled from grace in her effort to master the machine she named Gladys. "A good many people thought I could not do it at my age," she reported; there were dire predictions that "I should break my bones" or "spoil my future." And by her own admission, the erstwhile Wisconsin tomboy (hobbled by hoopskirts and high heels since the age of sixteen) was "at more disadvantage than most, for I suffered from the sedentary habits of a lifetime."

Evidently those torpid tendencies were deeply ingrained indeed, for it took wobbly Willard three months of daily practice, assisted by a corps of muscular aides-de-camp, to steer her "saucy steed" on a straight and narrow course. But on January 20, 1894, a date she proudly proclaimed her "red-letter bicycle day," the triumph of woman over machine was complete. "I had learned all her kinks, sighed the self-satisfied scorcher, "had put a bridle in her teeth, and touched her smartly with the whip of victory." From that day on, those who tried to tell Willard that women belonged on pedestals rather than pedals were just spinning their wheels. "The world is wide," wrote the upright cyclist, "and I would not waste my life in friction when it could be turned into momentum."

FREEWHEELING FRANCES SANS HER BICYCLE

"I finally concluded that all failure was from a wobbling will rather than a wobbling wheel."

—F. W.

Eternally Appealing

For fifty long years, Louisiana litigant Myra Gaines pursued her claim to her father's estate, even going so far as to personally pen an allegedly

Isobel Knowles (dates unknown)
The Tide Turns

At the turn of the century, the typical not-quite-liberated boater still preferred to pose prettily in the bow, relegating the overwhelming role of oarsman to a more capable male companion. "Her business," noted one arbiter of aquatic etiquette, "is solely to talk to him...and let him take her whither he will. It is exactly the arrangement which all men, and most women, probably, prefer."

It was not, however, the sort of arrangement preferred by robust rower Isobel Knowles, who presented a dramatic case for self-steerage in "Two Girls and a Canoe," published in the October 1905 issue of *Cosmopolitan*. "I am an experienced canoeist," announced the hoydenish hobbyist, who added that she had dipped her oars in Florida lagoons, Atlantic currents, and the pristine mountain streams of the Northeast. "But nowhere," she asserted, "Have I enjoyed the sport as on the wild forest rivers of Canada."

Different strokes, as they say, for different folks. The courageous *Cosmo* girl went on to describe a harrowing episode on the remote reaches of Canada's Gastineau River particularly relished both by herself and an intrepid female companion. "Two days' travel from the nearest outpost of civilization," she wrote, "a sudden narrowing of the channel brought us to the head of a gorge down which the river tossed and roared angrily like a living thing." Gauging the current at ten miles an hour, Knowles knew there was no turning back against the powerful pull—and small hope of survival if they were swept into the maelstrom. The imperiled paddlers averted that particular tragedy by jumping ship, then successfully retrieved their canoe from the roiling waters downstream.

Numerous other magnificent misadventures were yet to unfold, including a dizzying downriver descent toward a row of partially submerged rocks. "Below us, the dashing spray, the circling eddies, the increasing clamor of the torrent, seemed to lure us as the call of a Lorelei to destruction," Knowles recalled; "So far as I could see, nothing human could prevent a drowning." But in the end, it was mortal muscle, not divine intervention, that brought the "two girls" up safe and sound at the foot of the rapids, "gasping from our effort, yet thrilling with the joy of it."

As to whether Knowles' account of her death-defying exploits (which, she noted rather racily, infused her with "an ecstasy of abandon") did more to help or hinder the cause of the lady canoeist, one must draw her own conclusions. "Canoe stunts," the *Ladies Home Journal* was to sniff in 1915, "are better left to the heroines of fiction, who do not need to come back to superintend anything so prosaic as a dinner."

Nonetheless, as the decorous Victorian era drifted into decline, fewer females would view flotation solely as a forum for flirtation, nor would they deem the guidance of a gentleman crucial to its enjoyment. No passive party in a picture hat, the hardiest of the new breed of boaters plunged headlong into turbulent torrents with scarcely a second thought. For her, it was preferable to risk life and limb in the wild white waters than to succumb to one of society's most insidious white lies: that a woman could not paddle her own canoe.

"All the instinct of revolt bubbles forth as I paddle away from civilization."

—I. K.

BIBLIOGRAPHY

Abir-Am, Pnina G. and Dorinda Outram, eds. *Uneasy Careers and Intimate Lives*. New Brunswick, New Jersey: Rutgers University Press, 1987.

Adams, Abby. *An Uncommon Scold*. New York: Simon & Schuster, 1989.

Aikman, Duncan. *Calamity Jane and the Lady Wildcats*. New York: Henry Holt & Company, 1927.

Altrocchi, Julia. *The Spectacular San Franciscans*. New York: E.P. Dutton, 1949.

Anthony, Carl Sferrazza. *First Ladies*. New York: William Morrow & Company, Inc., 1990.

Armitage, Susan and Elizabeth Jameson. *The Women's West*. Norman, Oklahoma: University of Oklahoma Press, 1987.

Atherton, Gertrude. *Can Women Be Gentlemen?* Boston: Houghton Mifflin, 1938.

Ayer, Margaret Hubbard and Isabella Taves. *The Three Lives of Harriet Hubbard Ayer*. Philadelphia: J.B. Lippincott, 1957.

Banner, Lois. *American Beauty*. New York: Alfred A. Knopf, 1983.

Barnhart, Jacqueline Baker. *The Fair but Frail*. Reno: University of Nevada Press, 1986.

Benfey, Christopher. *Emily Dickinson*. New York: George Braziller, Inc., 1986.

Benson, Maxine. *Martha Maxwell*. Lincoln, Nebraska: University of Nebraska Press, 1986.

Berson, Misha. *The San Francisco Stage*. San Francisco: San Francisco Performing Arts Library and Museum, 1989.

Birmingham, Stephen. *The Grandes Dames*. New York: Simon & Schuster, 1982.

Black, Martha Louise. *Martha Black*. Bothell, Washington: Alaska Northwest Books, 1976.

Blashfield, Jean F. *Hellraisers, Heroines, and Holy Women*. New York: St. Martin's Press, 1981.

Brown, Arnold. *Lizzie Borden*. Nashville, Tennessee: Rutledge Hill Press, 1991.

Brown, Dee. *The Gentle Tamers: Women of the Old Wild West*. Lincoln, Nebraska: University of Nebraska Press, 1958.

Burke, John. *Duet in Diamonds: The Flamboyant Saga of Lillian Russell and Diamond Jim Brady in America's Gilded Age*. New York: G.P. Putnam's Sons, 1972.

Cayleff, Susan. *The Water-Cure Movement and Women's Health*. Philadelphia: Temple University Press, 1987.

Chopin, Kate. *The Awakening*. New York: G.P. Putnam's Sons, 1964.

Cleaveland, Agnes Morley. *No Life for a Lady*. Lincoln, Nebraska: University of Nebraska Press, 1977.

Cooper, Courtney Ryley. *Annie Oakley*. New York: Duffield & Company, 1927.

Cooper, Jilly and Tom Hartman. *Violets and Vinegar*. New York: Stein & Day, 1982.

Crocker, Aimee. *And I'd Do It Again*. New York: Coward-McCann, 1936.

Daniel, Pete and Raymond Smock. *A Talent for Detail: The Photographs of Miss Frances Benjamin Johnston*. New York: Harmony Books, 1974.

Drago, Harry Sinclair. *Notorious Ladies of the Frontier, Volume I.* New York: Ballantine Books, 1969.

Duberman, Martin, Martha Vicinus, and George Chauncey, Jr., eds. *Hidden from History.* New York: Penguin Books, 1989.

Dunlap, Carol. *California People.* Salt Lake City: Peregrine Smith Books, 1982.

Edmonds, S. Emma E. *Nurse and Spy in the Union Army.* Hartford, Connecticut: W.S. Williams & Co., 1865.

Ehrenreich, Barbara, and English, Deirdre. *For Her Own Good: 150 Years of the Experts' Advice to Women.* Garden City, New York: Anchor Press/Doubleday, 1978.

Faderman, Lillian. *Surpassing the Love of Men.* New York: William Morrow & Company, Inc., 1981.

_____. *Odd Girls and Twilight Lovers.* New York: Columbia University Press, 1991.

Fadiman, Clifton, ed. *The Little, Brown Book of Anecdotes.* Boston: Little, Brown & Company, 1985.

Forbes, Malcolm and Jeff Bloch. *Women Who Made a Difference.* New York: Simon & Schuster, 1990.

Fox-Genovese, Elizabeth. *Within the Plantation Household.* Chapel Hill: The University of North Carolina Press, 1988.

Freibert, Lucy M. and Barbara A. White, eds. *Hidden Hands.* New Brunswick, New Jersey: Rutgers University Press, 1985.

Fuller, Loie. *Fifteen Years of a Dancer's Life.* Boston: Small, Maynard & Company, 1913.

Fuller, Margaret. *Woman in the Nineteenth Century.* New York: W.W. Norton & Company, 1971.

Gattey, Charles Neilson. *The Bloomer Girls.* New York: Coward-McCann, Inc., 1967.

Gentry, Curt. *The Madams of San Francisco*. Garden City, New York: Doubleday & Co., 1964.

Gilman, Charlotte Perkins. *The Yellow Wallpaper and Other Writings*. New York: Bantam Books, 1989.

Glenn, Constance W. and Leland Rice. *Frances Benjamin Johnston: Women of Class and Station*. Long Beach, California: California State University Press, 1979.

Gordon, Mark. *Once Upon A City*. San Francisco: Don't Call It Frisco Press, 1988.

Gover, C. Jane. *The Positive Image: Women Photographers in Turn of the Century America*. Albany, New York: State University of New York Press, 1988.

Gray, Dorothy. *Women of the West*. Millbrae, California: Les Femmes, 1976.

Grier, Barbara and Coletta Reid, eds. *Lesbian Lives*. Oakland, California: Diana Press, 1976.

Griffin, Lynne and Kelly McCann. *The Book of Women: 300 Notable Women History Passed By*. Holbrook, Massachusetts: Bob Adams, Inc., 1992.

Hellerstein, Erna Olafson, Leslie Parker Hume and Karen M. Offen, eds. *Victorian Women*. Redwood City, California: Stanford University Press, 1981.

Herr, Pamela. *Jessie Benton Frémont*. New York: Franklin Watts, 1987.

Holdredge, Helen. *Mammy Pleasant*. New York: G.P. Putnam's Sons, 1953.

_____. *Firebelle Lillie*. New York: Meredith Press, 1967.

Howell, Reet. *Her Story in Sport*. West Point, New York: Leisure Press, 1982.

James, Edward T., Janet Wilson James, and Paul S. Boyer, eds. *Notable American Women 1607–1950*. Cambridge, Massachusetts: Belknap Press, 1971.

Kendall, Elizabeth. *Where She Danced*. New York: Alfred A. Knopf, 1979.

Kraditor, Aileen, ed. *Up from the Pedestal*. New York: The New York Times Book Company, 1975.

Leach, Joseph. *Bright Particular Star: The Life & Times of Charlotte Cushman*. New Haven: Yale University Press, 1970.

Leider, Emily Wortis. *California's Daughter: Gertrude Atherton and Her Times*. Redwood City, California: Stanford University Press, 1991.

Levy, Joann. *They Saw the Elephant: Women in the California Gold Rush*. Hamden, Connecticut: The Shoe String Press, 1990.

Lewis, Oscar. *Bonanza Inn*. New York: Alfred A. Knopf, 1939.

Long, Priscilla. *Mother Jones, Woman Organizer*. Boston: The South End Press, 1976.

Longford, Elizabeth. *Eminent Victorian Women*. London: Weidenfeld & Nicolson, 1981.

Luchetti, Cathy and Carol Olwell. *Women of the West*. St. George, Utah: Antelope Island Press, 1982.

Martin, Cy. *Whiskey and Wild Women*. New York: Hart Publishing Company, Inc., 1974.

Moffat, Mary Jane and Charlotte Painter, eds. *Revelations: Diaries of Women*. New York: Random House, 1974.

Monk, Maria. *The Awful Disclosures of Maria Monk, As Exhibited in a Narrative of Her Sufferings during a Residence of Five Years as a Novice, and Two Years as a Black Nun, in the Hôtel Dieu Nunnery at Montreal*. London: Houlston & Stoneman, 1851.

Muhlenfeld, Elisabeth. *Mary Boykin Chestnut*. Baton Rouge: Louisiana State University Press, 1981.

Niemi, Judith and Barbara Wieser, eds. *Rivers Running Free*. Minneapolis: Bergamot Books, 1987.

Peavy, Linda and Ursula Smith. *Women Who Changed Things*. New York: Charles Scribner's Sons, 1983.

Pember, Phoebe Yates. *A Southern Woman's Story*. Jackson, Tenness: McCowat-Mercer Press, Inc., 1959.

Pyron, Darden Asbury. *Southern Daughter: The Life of Margaret Mitchell*. New York: Oxford University Press, 1991.

Rappaport, Doreen, ed. *American Women: Their Lives in Their Words*. New York: Thomas Y. Crowell, 1990.

Ray, Grace Ernestine. *Wiley Women of the West*. San Antonio, Texas: The Naylor Company, 1972.

Reiter, Joan Swallow. *The Old West: The Women*. Alexandria, Virginia: Time-Life Books, 1978.

Richards, Dell. *Lesbian Lists*. Boston: Alyson Publications, Inc., 1990.

Robbins, Millie. *Tales of Love and Hate in Old San Francisco*. San Francisco: Chronicle Books, 1971.

Ross, Ishbel. *Charmers and Cranks*. New York: Harper & Row, 1965.

Scott, Anne Firor. *The Southern Lady*. Chicago: University of Chicago Press, 1970.

Smith-Rosenberg, Carroll. *Disorderly Conduct: Visions of Gender in Victorian America*. New York: Alfred A. Knopf, 1985.

Spiering, Frank. *Lizzie*. New York: Random House, 1984.

Stage, Sarah. *Female Complaints: Lydia Pinkham and the Business of Women's Medicine*. New York: W.W. Norton & Company, 1979.

Stern, Madeleine B. *We the Women*. New York: Schulte Publishing Company, 1963.

Strouse, Jean. *Alice James*. Boston: Houghton Mifflin Company, 1980.

Toth, Emily. *Kate Chopin*. New York: William Morrow & Company, Inc., 1990.

Truman, Margaret. *Women of Courage*. New York: William Morrow & Company, Inc., 1976.

Uglow, Jennifer S. and Frances Hinton, eds. *The Continuum Dictionary of Women's Biography*. New York: The Continuum Publishing Company, 1982.

Vare, Ethlie Ann and Greg Ptacek. *Mothers of Invention*. New York: William Morrow & Company, Inc. 1987.

Wallace, Irving. *The Twenty-Seventh Wife*. New York: Simon & Schuster, 1961.

Wallace, Irving and Amy Wallace. *The Two*. New York: Simon & Schuster, 1978.

Wells, Evelyn. *Champagne Days in San Francisco*. New York: D. Appleton-Century Company, 1939.

Wheelwright, Julie. *Amazons and Military Maids*. London: Pandora Press, 1989

Whitton, Mary Ormsbee. *These Were the Women*. New York: Hastings House, 1954.

Wiley, Belle Irvin. *Confederate Women*. Westport, Connecticut: Greenwood Press, 1975.

Willard, Frances. *How I Learned to Ride the Bicycle*. Sunnyvale, California: Fair Oaks Publishing Company, 1991.

Woodward, Helen Beal. *The Bold Women*. New York: Farrar, Straus & Young, 1953.

Zahniser, J.D., ed. *And Then She Said...*, *Vols. 1 and 2*. St. Paul, Minnesota: Caillech Press, 1989.

ABOUT THE AUTHOR

Autumn Stephens was born in a New Mexico mining community whose population began to dwindle shortly after her arrival (though she swears this was mere coincidence) and finally faded from the map altogether. She spent the rest of her childhood in Eugene, Oregon. Initially, she intended to become a psychologist, but when she noticed that her introductory psych classes at Stanford University tended to focus on the behavior of rats rather than that of human beings, she signed up as a Creative Writing major instead. During several subsequent years as an afterhours creative writer; daytime wage slave, Stephens worked as a medical coder, a phone sex script writer, a composer of fraudulent Tarot prognostications, and something called a "special investigator" for the State Bar of California. More than any other experience, however, her stint as an old fashioned legal secretary (among other absurdities, the job involved the daily composition of a heart-healthy salad for a high-maintenance male boss) honed the deliciously snide feminist sensibility which informs Stephens' writing today. (Well, okay, growing up more or less concurrently with the women's movement of the 1960s and 1970s helped too.) Stephens is the author of the popular Wild Women books published by Conari Press, including *Wild Women*, *Wild Women in the White House*, *Wild Words from Wild Women*, *Loose Cannons*, *Drama Queens*, and *Out of the Mouths of Babes*. Stephens also freelances for magazines, reviews women's writing for the San Francisco Chronicle, and enjoys an entirely attorney free lifestyle. Currently, she lives in Berkeley, California, a city that she would like better were it not for an uncharacteristically restrictive ordinance against raising miniature pigs in one's backyard. Her hobbies are sleeping and reading trashy celebrity magazines.

Mango Publishing, established in 2014, publishes an eclectic list of books by diverse authors—both new and established voices—on topics ranging from business, personal growth, women's empowerment, LGBTQ studies, health, and spirituality to history, popular culture, time management, decluttering, lifestyle, mental wellness, aging, and sustainable living. We were recently named 2019 *and* 2020's #1 fastest growing independent publisher by *Publishers Weekly*. Our success is driven by our main goal, which is to publish high quality books that will entertain readers as well as make a positive difference in their lives.

Our readers are our most important resource; we value your input, suggestions, and ideas. We'd love to hear from you—after all, we are publishing books for you!

Please stay in touch with us and follow us at:

Facebook: Mango Publishing
Twitter: @MangoPublishing
Instagram: @MangoPublishing
LinkedIn: Mango Publishing
Pinterest: Mango Publishing

Newsletter: mangopublishinggroup.com/newsletter

Join us on Mango's journey to reinvent publishing, one book at a time.